JULIUS CAESAR, CEO

JULIUS CAESAR, CEO

6 PRINCIPLES TO GUIDE & INSPIRE MODERN LEADERS

ALAN AXELROD

STERLING
New York

STERLING
New York

An Imprint of Sterling Publishing
387 Park Avenue South

STERLING and the distinctive Sterling logo are registered trademarks of Sterling Publishing Co., Inc.

ISBN 978-1-4027-8484-2

Library of Congress Cataloging-in-Publication Data

Axelrod, Alan, 1952-
 Julius Caesar, CEO : 6 principles to guide & inspire modern leaders / Alan Axelrod.
  p. cm.
 Includes index.
 ISBN 978-1-4027-8484-2
 1. Leadership. 2. Caesar, Julius. 3. Chief executive officers. I. Title.
 HD57.7.A9584 2012
 658.4'092--dc23
                           2012000728

Distributed in Canada by Sterling Publishing
c/o Canadian Manda Group, 165 Dufferin Street
Toronto, Ontario, Canada M6K 3H6
Distributed in the United Kingdom by GMC Distribution Services
Castle Place, 166 High Street, Lewes, East Sussex, England BN7 1XU
Distributed in Australia by Capricorn Link (Australia) Pty. Ltd.
P.O. Box 704, Windsor, NSW 2756, Australia

For information about custom editions, special sales, and premium and corporate purchases, please contact Sterling Special Sales at 800-805-5489 or specialsales@sterlingpublishing.com.

Manufactured in the United States of America

2 4 6 8 10 9 7 5 3 1

www.sterlingpublishing.com

FRONTISPIECE: Julius Caesar Statue on the Via Imperiali, Rome.

PICTURE CREDITS:
ii: Statue of Julius Caesar in Turin (c) Shutterstock/ArturKo
v: Courtesy the Library of Congress Prints & Photographs Division, LC-USZC4-2833, Andrea Andreani, *Triunph(us) Caesari*s (*The triumph of Julius Caesar*), plate 9, ca. 1598

Chapter openers: Vintage engraving from 1857 photograph, © iStockphoto/Duncan Walker

For Anita and Ian

CONTENTS

Introduction
The Noblest Roman of Them All

"O Julius Caesar! Thou art mighty yet!"

~ William Shakespeare, *Julius Caesar*, V, iii

Flowing lazily between Cesena and Rimini in northeastern Italy, the Rubicon is a river remarkable in neither length, width, nor depth. In crossing it in 49 BCE, however, Julius Caesar entered history, popular culture, and the course of Western civilization not only as an inspired military thinker and leader, enlightened dictator, brilliant orator, statesman, writer, architect of empire, and self-made (though by design uncrowned) emperor, but also as the archetypal chief executive officer.

For inconsiderable though the river is, the Rubicon was no ordinary body of water. In 49 BCE, it divided northern Italy– Cisalpine Gaul, a portion of the vast province Caesar consolidated and controlled–from Rome proper, which was governed by the Senate and dominated by the powerful Pompey the Great, formerly Caesar's ally and fellow triumvir (in effect, one of three political bosses), now his arch rival. A solemn law barred any Roman general from leading an army out of the province to which he was assigned. So when Caesar crossed the Rubicon, he defied the majesty of Rome, pitting his six-thousand-soldier vanguard against the far vaster legions that answered to Pompey and the Senate. Caesar's act was of such moment that "crossing the Rubicon" became idiomatic shorthand for making any decision of the highest importance, entailing great risk and the possibility of great reward, and from which, once the decision is acted upon, there is no turning back.

If Caesar's crossing the Rubicon—considered as the sum of everything that had motivated it and the source of everything that proceeded from it—is the quintessential act of decision making, so decision making is the ultimate and essential business of the CEO. As the leader who chose to cross that modest river so rich with cost and consequence, Caesar is among the first and perhaps the greatest of executives: an iconic CEO.

■

If language is any measure, Julius Caesar set a cross-cultural, pan-historical standard of leadership. Not long after he was assassinated, the name *Caesar* became a synonym for ruler and has been adopted in the German language (*Kaiser* is pronounced exactly like *Caesar* in classical Latin, with a hard *c*), in Russian and other Slavonic languages (*Czar* is a monosyllabic elision of *Caesar*), and in various languages of the Islamic world (*Qaysar*).

Noble Ancestry, Populist Present

Caesar was born on July 13, 100 BCE, into a noble family that had seen better days. His gens (roughly equivalent to his clan), the Julii, were patricians, meaning that they traced their pedigree to the original aristocracy of Rome and even to the goddess Venus. During the fourth century BCE, many of the original patrician families of Rome intermarried with the most prosperous plebian (commoner) families, so that, by the time of Caesar's birth, merely possessing patrician blood no longer guaranteed a place in the ruling class. There was still a politically, socially, culturally, emotionally, and economically profound division between those who considered themselves noble (a category that was no longer purely patrician, however) and those who were frankly plebian (had no patrician blood in their lineage), but, ever since the fourth century, leadership was becoming as much a matter of politics as of class, let alone birthright. Indeed, politics and heredity were often at odds in Roman government and culture, sometimes violently so. If patrician blood could be an asset in the political arena, it could also be a liability, since one of the most important and powerful political offices in the Roman Republic, that of tribune—the voice of the plebs—was entirely closed to the patrician class. The one commodity that *could* readily overcome the negative aspects of noble birth was money. Roman political life was fueled by cash, which was used for everything from staging crowd-pleasing public spectacles to buying influence, and to giving bribes, a practice that seems to have had semi-legal status. The Julii Caesares—to use both their gens name and their family name—had had big money at one time, but not for a long time.

It was true that Julius Caesar's father, whose name was also Julius Caesar, significantly improved the family's flagging economic position by marrying Aurelia Cotta, the daughter of a former consul. By the time his son was born, the Julii Caesares were by no means impoverished, but neither were they powerful, influential, or socially distinguished. They are best described as being of the middling sort.

Gaius Julius Caesar (following Roman tradition, the first name was personal, the middle denoted *gens* ["clan"], and the last, called the *cognomen*, was a kind of family nickname passed from father to son) was born in a modest dwelling in an unfashionable, even rundown, Roman neighborhood called Subura. While it was just a short walk to the Forum, the center of Roman political life, Subura was a low-lying, miasmic district inhabited by common tradesmen, foreigners—including a large number of Jews—and a small Roman legion of prostitutes. When Julius Caesar was eleven years old, his uncle, Sextus Caesar, served as consul (one of two high magistrates, who were elected yearly and governed together by consensus) for the year 91. The following year, a distant cousin, Lucius Caesar, was likewise elected consul, as was his son, also named Lucius, in 64.

An action the first Lucius took as consul helped shape the direction of the young Caesar's politics. The year 90 BCE saw a rebellion of certain non-Roman states in Italy provoked by Rome's stubborn refusal to extend to their residents coveted Roman citizenship. The restriction had been sponsored by the noble party in the Senate, the so-called Optimates, against whom Lucius Caesar acted by pushing through the Senate an emergency act that granted citizenship to all Italian states that had either not joined the rebellion or that agreed to return to the Roman fold. This put Lucius in the anti-Optimate party, often called the Populares, and thus Gaius Julius Caesar came of age in a middling patrician household with marked populist political leanings. This orientation was strengthened by the fact that his much-adored aunt, Julia, was the wife of Gaius Marius, leader of the Populares.

At home in Subura, it was another woman, Aurelia, his mother, who most influenced Gaius Julius. The mark she made on history—as a sharp, cultured, politically savvy woman entirely devoted to her only son (she also had at least two daughters)—is much more vivid than the obscure trace left by the boy's father. He served as a magistrate and as an official in an Asian province, positions that kept him far from home and family. His death, in 85 BCE, came at home, however, and under the most homely of circumstances. While putting on his shoes one morning, he fell dead. His son was sixteen at the time.

Because Aurelia haled from well-to-do parents, the death of the senior Julius Caesar did not leave the family destitute, and, within a year of his father's death, young Caesar (doubtless through the influence of his mother and aunt) was named the new high priest of Jupiter. It was a significant honor, but it carried no salary, and he and Aurelia remained in humble Subura. In the years to come, virtually everything Caesar would do to advance his political career had to be financed with borrowed money. Debt would be his perpetual companion.

Launching a Career and Defying Death

Politics, Caesar knew, was expensive, but, as a youth and a young man, he seems never to have seriously considered any other vocation. He was betrothed to a wealthy young woman named Cossutia, and it is even possible that he actually married her shortly after the death of his father. Nevertheless, the union—whether by betrothal or marriage—did not last long, and in 84 BCE, after he had turned eighteen, Caesar married Cornelia. Among Romans who intended to rise to prominence, a marriage could make or break a career. Cornelia's father, Lucius Cornelius Cinna, was a nobleman who nevertheless collaborated with Gaius Marius, the leader of the Populares. Already Marius's nephew, Caesar made a choice of wife that ratified his identification with the anti-Optimate party. Before the end of the year, however, Cinna was stoned to death in a mutiny of his own soldiers. Hearing of this, the former consul of Rome, prominent general, and towering Optimate leader Lucius Cornelius Sulla, eager to fill the power vacuum, returned to Rome from the eastern provinces, where he had successfully put down a series of anti-Roman revolts.

Sulla believed that the popularist reforms of Cinna had undermined the Roman Republic, and he sought to restore order by returning Rome to conservative (indeed, reactionary) Optimate governance. Eager for stability, the Senate, toward the end of 82 or the start of 81 BCE, appointed Sulla dictator "for the making of laws and for the settling of the constitution." The popular assembly not only ratified the Senate's decision, but also set no expiration date on the dictatorship. This shattered the time-honored Roman tradition of withholding ultimate authority from any single consul, and historians have seen in it the precedent by which Julius Caesar would himself later assume sole dictatorial authority.

But that moment was years in the future. In many ways, Sulla resembled the kind of totalitarian dictator the twentieth century would make all too familiar. He carried out a purge of those he identified as enemies of the state, formally ordering some fifteen hundred nobles to their deaths and probably sanctioning the murder of many more. (Historians believe that the political killings may have amounted to a total of some nine thousand.) Corruption both accompanied and drove the terror, as Sulla and his allies reaped the rewards of mountains of state-confiscated wealth.

Having literally wed himself to Sulla's opposition, Caesar was a prime target of the purge. Sulla ordered him stripped of whatever inheritance might be due him and also of his wife's dowry—which was far more considerable than the inheritance—as well as his recently conferred priesthood. Sulla did, however, yield to the pleas of influential members of Aurelia's family to spare the young man's life, though he did so with utmost reluctance, warning that "In this Caesar there are many Mariuses," a pointed reference to Gaius Marius, the leader of the Populares, who had died (of natural causes) in 86 BCE.

One thing Sulla refused to back down on was his demand that Caesar divorce Cinna's daughter, Cornelia. Had the young man truly been the kind of blatant political opportunist many would later accuse him of being, he would have readily bowed to Sulla's demand. Instead, he defiantly refused and sought a way out of Rome by entering the army on the staff of the propraetor (a combination military commander and magistrate) of Roman Asia, Marcus Thermus. In this capacity, Caesar immediately departed for service in the province of Asia and then in Cilicia, Asia Minor. Thermus ordered him to Bithynia (a strategically situated kingdom adjoining the Bosporus Strait, the Sea of Marmara, and the Black Sea) to obtain ships from King Nicomedes of Bithynia to aid in the siege of Mytilene on the island of Lesbos. Caesar performed this mission so well and displayed such conspicuous heroism in the subsequent assault on Mytilene that he was awarded the honor of a

Civic Crown. Nevertheless, the errand to Nicomedes gave rise to rumors of a tryst with that king. Roman society was quite tolerant of homosexuality, provided that one was not discovered playing a submissive role in the affair. Caesar was portrayed as having sexually submitted to the king, and taunts of his having become the "Queen of Bithynia" would dog him for the rest of his life.

Despite these potentially career-wrecking rumors, Caesar benefited from his military experience. Not only was martial glory a more promising route to political prominence than the priestly office that had been taken away from him, but the Civic Crown was a significant distinction for a youth of nineteen. When Sulla died in 78 BCE, Caesar not only felt safe enough to return to Rome, he was able to do so not as a fugitive but as a military hero.

Back in Rome, with neither dowry nor inheritance, Caesar turned to the practice of law to make a living. He quickly proved to be as able an advocate as he was a soldier and drew much approval for his well-reasoned but impassioned oratory in vigorously prosecuting a series of former governors notorious for corruption. Always seeking to raise the bar of his own performance, Caesar took ship for Rhodes in 75 BCE to formally study rhetoric and oratory under Apollonius Molon, a world-renowned professor of these subjects. As Lesson 67, "Refuse Victimhood," narrates, Caesar was captured en route by pirates, from whom he not only ransomed himself but against whom he exacted bloody vengeance. Although he was a private citizen of Rome and held neither military nor civil office, Caesar, once he was ransomed, managed to raise a naval force and then assume command of it in the swift capture of the pirates. He boldly ordered local officials to crucify his prisoners, and although he possessed no judicial authority whatsoever, they complied without argument.

The Climb Begins

On his return to Rome after his adventure with the pirates, Caesar discovered that he had been made a pontifex, a member of the

College of Pontiffs, one of four priestly colleges in ancient Rome. This politico-religious office was quickly augmented by his election to a military tribuneship. Together, these positions gave Caesar sufficient clout to form an alliance with Gnaeus Pompeius—later known as Gnaeus Pompeius Magnus, Pompey the Great—who, having risen to power as one of Sulla's lieutenants, switched allegiance to the Populares after the dictator's death. Together, Caesar and Pompey worked to dismantle the reactionary constitutional changes Sulla had made.

Caesar soon parlayed his pontificate and tribuneship into higher office, when he was elected in the year 69 (or possibly 68) as quaestor. An office with supervisory responsibility over the Roman treasury and general financial affairs, quaestor was the first major step in the so-called *cursus honorum*—the "course of offices" by which aspiring political leaders rose to successively greater authority in the Roman Republic.

Later in 69, both Caesar's aunt Julia and his wife, Cornelia, died, occasioning from Caesar masterful funeral orations that elicited significant public sympathy and political approval, even as they further identified him with the popularist cause of Cinna and Marius (see Lesson 68, "Take *Every* Opportunity to Broadcast Your Brand"). After serving his quaestorship in the province of Hispania Ulterior ("Farther Spain," encompassing modern Andalusia and Portugal), Caesar returned to Rome in 67 and married Pompeia, a distant relative of Pompey, whose father was a former consul and whose mother was the daughter of Sulla.

Caesar continued his upward progress through the cursus honorum with his election as one of the curule aediles for 65 BCE. Each year, two aediles were chosen from among the plebs and two from the nobility (these latter two were called curule aediles). All four had charge of maintaining public buildings, of maintaining public order, and of managing public festivals. It was in the latter role that Caesar truly distinguished himself, contributing his own lavishly borrowed money to mount festivals guaranteed to impress, delight, and generally please the public (see Lesson 1, "Gamble/ Invest").

Having, as curule aedile, built popular support as well as a staggering personal debt, Caesar next gained election to the exulted office of pontifex maximus, high priest of the College of Pontiffs, in 63 BCE (see Lesson 83, "Aim Higher"). In this same year, he made himself both conspicuous and controversial by arguing against Consul Marcus Tullius Cicero by pleading for clemency in the case of certain men accused of plotting against the Republic in the infamous Catiline Conspiracy (see Lesson 19, "Temper Policy with Pragmatism").

Despite, or perhaps because of, the controversial position Caesar took against Cicero, he was elected a praetor for 62 BCE. Now holding an office that was the equivalent of the highest magistrate of the Republic, Caesar grew increasingly confident of his rise—until a bizarre scandal threatened to topple him.

As the end of Caesar's praetorship year drew to a close in December 62, one Publius Clodius Pulcher, a radical popularist, apparently began an affair with Pompeia. As if this weren't bad enough (adultery was tolerated in Rome; outright cuckoldry, however, was mercilessly ridiculed), Clodius, disguising himself as a woman, crashed the Bona Dea, which was held at Caesar's official residence, the Regia, and was presided over by Pompeia and Caesar's mother, Aurelia. This sacred ceremony of the "Good Goddess" cult was a strictly female occasion, from which all men were rigorously excluded. When a servant girl discovered Clodius's disguise, a spectacular scandal erupted. It not only monopolized public discourse, but prompted Caesar to divorce Pompeia. He neither demanded nor sought positive proof of his wife's adultery or of her complicity in Clodius's intrusion into the Bona Dea ceremony. He simply ended the marriage, with the notable declaration that "Caesar's wife must be above suspicion."

Rise to Consul and the First Triumvirate

Caesar prepared to leave Rome after the expiration of his praetorship to take up his assignment as governor of Hispania Ulterior for 61–60 BCE. It was not the lingering effects of the Bona Dea scandal that threatened to stop him from leaving the city, but the long arm of his many creditors, who refused to let him depart until his friend and ally Crassus posted bail in the amount of 25 percent of his total debt. That Crassus willingly put up a staggering amount of money suggests the magnitude of confidence Caesar's allies eagerly invested in him.

And Crassus by no means misplaced his faith. During his Spanish sojourn, Caesar led military campaigns just beyond the northwest frontier of his assigned province, accumulating spoils that not only made a respectable dent in his debts, but enriched his soldiers (winning their loyalty as no mere succession of victories or patriotic speeches ever could), and still left him with a bundle of cash to pour into the Roman Republic's coffers. Thus enriched, Caesar was now in an excellent position to return to Rome and stand for election to the highest office in the cursus honorum: the consulship of the year 59 BCE.

Not only was the office of consul a position of high honor and power, it carried with it the prospect of a most lucrative provincial governorship to follow. It was thus a plum coveted by many, and bribery and other forms of chicanery were liberally employed to pluck it. The Senate, dominated by Optimates, sought to make the consulship of 59 unpalatable to the likes of Caesar by linking it not to governing some rich province, but to the supervision of forests and cattle trails in Italy—a dismal and profitless job. Worse, to stand for election as Caesar's co-consul (two consuls were elected yearly and had to govern by consensus), the Senate promoted Marcus Calpurnius Bibulus, an outspoken political foe. Yet such was Caesar's popularity—and his own skill and daring in the judicious application of bribery—that he achieved election.

He had fought so hard to obtain the consulship that Caesar was determined to gain more than a year of influence. He reached out to Pompey, who, having returned from a brilliantly successful military expedition in Rome's eastern provinces, sought to build his power base among the veterans of his now-disbanded army by securing land allotments for them. The Senate thwarted him in this, however, whereupon Caesar proposed joining political forces and co-opting Rome's third most powerful populist, Marcus Licinius Crassus, to create a three-man syndicate of what can only be described as political bosses. Known to history as the First Triumvirate, this coalition had no official government standing, but was very powerful nonetheless. What is more, in a stroke of true political genius, Caesar ensured that he would be effectively the linchpin of the triumvirate. Pompey and Crassus had both risen during the reign of Sulla, but the two had become political enemies. Caesar mediated between them, holding together the triumvirate and driving it forward. As for Pompey, he effectively ratified his partnership with Caesar by marrying, in 59 BCE, Caesar's only daughter, Julia. This same year, Caesar himself was married for a third time, to Calpurnia Pisonis, daughter of Lucius Calpurnius Piso Caesoninus, who would become consul following Caesar in 58 BCE.

In Power

Consul Julius Caesar wasted no time in introducing before the Senate a land reform bill that distributed Roman public lands throughout Italy, beginning with a generous allotment to Pompey's veterans. The Senate dragged its feet, the bill was vetoed by three tribunes of the plebs, and Consul Bibulus introduced his own delaying tactics (see Lesson 2, "Look for a Way Around"), but, in the end, Caesar exposed Bibulus as a hollow would-be tyrant and then stirred Pompey's veterans to riot. Between growing popular support, outrage against Bibulus and the Senate, and fear of civil unrest, the bill was passed. Rome's Italian public lands were distributed, and hitherto dispossessed farmers, who had been crowding Rome and posing a continual threat to civil stability, were now peacefully settled on their own farms.

Caesar followed this historic land reform with another momentous bill settling much of the eastern provinces that Pompey had conquered. Passage of this legislation was achieved largely through Caesar's skilled negotiation with Publius Vatinius, tribune of the people. This was followed by an important piece of legislation providing a schedule of judicial punishments for corrupt provincial governors.

The tribune Vatinius subsequently sponsored another bill of supreme importance to Caesar. Instead of saddling him with the supervision of forests and cattle trails in Italy, Vatinius proposed giving Caesar nothing less than Cisalpine Gaul (the Roman province bounded by the Alps, Apennines, and Adriatic) and Illyricum (encompassing the northern portion of modern Albania and Croatia). Caesar would be assigned to govern this province until February 28, 54 BCE. Not only did the Senate enact the bill, but when the governor-designate of Transalpine Gaul (Gallia Narbonensis or Gallia Transalpina, encompassing what are today Languedoc and Provence in the south of France) died before assuming office, Caesar was assigned this vast region as well. Taken together, he now had an unprecedented opportunity to create an empire and to build personal power. The tribes of Cisalpine Gaul, many of which already professed themselves allies of Rome, were a large pool from which Caesar could recruit the legions that he would lead into Transalpine Gaul, a territory (as he saw it) ripe for conquests beyond the Roman Republic's farthest frontier.

The Conquest of Gaul

The pacification of Cisalpine Gaul and the conquest of Transalpine Gaul occupied Caesar from 58 to 50 BCE and was the central masterpiece of his military and political career. During this period, Julius Caesar pushed the empire of the Roman Republic as far as the left bank of the Rhine, and, what is more, thoroughly subjugated the region, so that it remained a secure province throughout the turbulent period of Roman civil warfare that began in 49 BCE and continued through 31.

The pacification and conquest of Gaul was a magnificently entrepreneurial achievement. Caesar had hardly been given vast, let alone limitless, military resources. In almost every campaign and every battle, his forces were significantly outnumbered and often underequipped, overmatched in manpower as well as arms by the Gauls, Celts, and Germans. The successes Caesar enjoyed were due to a combination of his leadership and his skill in tactics and strategy, plus the tradition of military discipline instilled in the Roman legions and the Roman mastery of large-scale civil engineering. Most of the lessons in the chapters that follow in this book are drawn from the extraordinary span of ancient history and matchless military leadership that is the period of the Gallic War.

Modern historians tend to see the conquest of Gaul in global terms. Their narratives are the verbal equivalent of great animated maps, in which the influence of Rome is depicted as spreading like the light of civilization or a bloody stain, depending on the sensibility of the writer. To be sure, the conquest of Gaul changed the world and created history. Caesar himself probably saw the conquest more as a means than as an end. His objective was certainly to expand the sphere of Roman hegemony, but his even greater goal was to acquire the glory that would give him the power, the prestige, and (not least of all) the plunder to remodel Rome and its imperial holdings under his own leadership.

Shakespeare is the greatest but far from the only author who asked of Caesar's conquering ways the question that had first been put into Latin by the stern Roman censor Lucius Cassius Longinus Ravilla more than a quarter century before Caesar had even been born: *Cui bono?* "Who benefits?"

Who benefited from Caesar's rise to power and his leadership of conquest? Was it Rome? The Western world? Or was it Gaius Julius Caesar? Caesar might have answered that it was all three, but what is certain is that he would have denied none of them. He felt no shame in coveting glory and exercising power.

Although the conquest of Gaul is addressed in many of the lessons presented in this book, it is helpful to begin here with an overview. At the back of the book, you will also find a Caesarian timeline, which summarizes the events of the Gallic War as well as the other milestones of Caesar's life.

When Caesar arrived in Gaul in 58 BCE, Rome's northwestern frontier was little changed from what it had been when it was established in 125. It was bounded by the Alps and ran down the left bank of the upper Rhône River as far as the Pyrenees, and then touched the southeastern foot of the Cévennes Mountains and encompassed the upper basin of the Garonne River, but stopped well short of the Atlantic shore.

Almost immediately, Caesar ventured beyond these long-established borderlands. His first major target was the Helvetii, who had made incursions into Gaul from their tribal territories in what is today central Switzerland. Next, he defeated Ariovistus, the highly skilled military chieftain of the Suebi (Suevi) tribe, who led a coalition of Germanic warriors eastward across the Rhine and into Gaul.

In the year 57 BCE, Caesar launched a major campaign against the fierce Belgic tribes, from the northern extremity of Gaul. At the same time, acting under Caesar's orders, Marcus Licinius Crassus pacified tribes in what are today Normandy and Brittany. This was followed in 56 by Caesar's own campaigns against the Veneti, a Celtic tribe centered in the southern portion of modern Brittany. Together with the Morini (who lived in the vicinity of the Straits of Dover) and the Menapii (resident along the south bank of the lower Rhine), the Veneti conducted a revolt that was vast in geographical scope. Caesar suppressed the Veneti with what was for him (up to this point) uncharacteristically genocidal thoroughness, but winter set in before he could finish his campaign against the Morini and Menapii. He returned to them with a vengeance during 55 BCE, virtually wiping them from the face of Europe.

It was in this year as well that Caesar stepped beyond the eastern boundary of Gaul, boldly bridging the Rhine just below the modern city of Koblenz for a lightning raid into Germany (see Lesson 29, "Cross the Rhine," and Lesson 30, "Cross the Rhine—in Style"). After this, he pushed in the opposite direction, crossing the treacherous English Channel to raid Britain—once in 55 BCE and a second time in 54—returning to northeastern Gaul to put down a major revolt that had broken out in his absence. He acted against rebellious tribes again in 53, and, yet again, threw a bridge across the Rhine for a second raid into Germany.

The most serious uprising Caesar faced in Gaul came in 52, when Vercingetorix, a chieftain of the Arverni (who lived in what is today the French Auvergne), united tribes in central Gaul in a massive offensive against the Romans, involving tens of thousands—perhaps as many as 330,000—warriors. Vercingetorix proved a highly capable commander of his enormous forces, which he used to execute a strategy of cutting off Caesar's legions from their sources of supply while also enforcing a scorched-earth policy to deprive them of local forage. In this approach, Vercingetorix showed genuine military insight. He understood that an invader's weakness is always supply and that an invading force is at all times vulnerable to being isolated and cut off. These weaknesses were his sources of leverage, whereas engaging the highly disciplined legions in pitched battles offered him no advantage, because doing so would play to the Romans' prodigious tactical strengths. Unfortunately for Vercingetorix, he was unable to universally enforce his strict scorched-earth measures on his fellow Gauls, and, at the culminating siege and Battle of Alesia (September 52), Vercingetorix was defeated. With his surrender, the possibility of a united Gallic insurrection ended (see Lesson 13, "Winner Take Nothing," and Lesson 89, "Invest in a Scarlet Cloak").

The winter of 52–51 BCE and the spring and summer of 51 saw lesser revolts, most notably among the Bellovaci, who lived between the Seine and Somme Rivers, near what is today Beauvais. Also, at Uxellodunum (believed to be the Puy d'Issolu on the Dordogne River) another force resisted the Romans until their water supply ran dry. By this time, Caesar was determined to teach would-be rebels the harshest lessons possible. He cut off the hands of those who survived the siege of Uxellodunum.

Dissolution of the Triumvirate

While conquering Gaul, Caesar did his best to stay in contact with the developing situation in Rome. Each year, he used the winter season, a time in which military operations were usually suspended, to leave Gaul and return to Italy, and he also saw to it that the proceeds from his Gallic campaign efficiently bought political influence back in Rome. Despite this, the triumvirate eroded. Pompey grew jealous of Caesar, and in Caesar's absence, Crassus and Pompey were increasingly at one another's throats. Caesar met with his partners at Luca (modern Lucca, Italy) in April 56 BCE and bought them off with favors. Pompey and Crassus were set to be voted in as co-consuls for the year 55. In turn, they would authorize the prolongation of Caesar's commission in Gaul. Crassus, in turn, would be given a five-year governorship of Syria, and Pompey would hold sway over Spain for five years. This settled, Crassus marched off to campaign in Parthia—only to die in battle in the year 53 BCE. This reduced the triumvirate to the duo of Caesar and Pompey. In 54, however, Pompey's wife, Julia, died, and without the bond of marriage tying him to Caesar, Pompey quickly veered away from Caesar and the Populares, concluding an alliance with the Optimates, a connection he deemed preferable to subordinating himself to Caesar.

Now Pompey conspired with the Senate to whittle away at Caesar's power. As the term of his governorship in Gaul was about to expire, Caesar knew that he was required by law to disband his army before returning to Rome to take up a second consulship. The problem was that in the interval between the disbanding of his army and the commencement of his consulship, he would be totally powerless and therefore completely vulnerable. This would not be so bad, provided that Pompey were subject to the same provision of disarmament; however, in 50 BCE, Consul Gaius Claudius Marcellus obtained Senate orders requiring Caesar to lay down his command while Pompey was allowed to retain his. This development triggered a series of complex political maneuvers, which culminated in Caesar's sending to the Senate a proposal that he and Pompey should be ordered to relinquish their commands simultaneously. The Senate found the tone of Caesar's message insolent and offensive and replied indignantly by declaring Caesar a public enemy if he should fail to renounce his command "by a date to be fixed" (see Lesson 34, "Defeat Doubt").

Crossing the Rubicon into Civil War

Roman law debarred any general from entering Rome proper with his army. As discussed in Lesson 34, "Defeat Doubt," Caesar's impasse with the Senate prompted him on January 10–11, 49 BCE, to cross the Rubicon, which divided his province of Cisalpine Gaul from Roman Italy. By this crossing, he broke the law and committed an act of civil war. Caesar hoped that it would preserve his power and save his life, but, even more, he sought to end the corrupt misgovernment of the entire Greco-Roman world by the Roman nobility and replace it with a strong government led not by a consensus of two consuls but by himself alone.

Caesar knew that crossing the Rubicon would mean civil war, but he had no desire to provoke what he feared would be a long and bloody conflict. Yet he saw no other alternative to his immediate demise followed by the somewhat slower death of Rome itself. His success in Gaul had made him so powerful that the corrupt old guard of Rome could think of nothing but destroying him. As for Pompey, his former ally, jealousy had driven him to side with the Senate.

The civil war began well for Caesar, who, in 49 BCE, pushed the Optimate army out of Italy and all the way to the eastern side of the Strait of Otranto. He then turned against the Pompeian army in Spain, and, after suffering a reverse at Dyrrachium (today Durrës, Albania), he dogged Pompey across the Adriatic and achieved a decisive victory at Pharsalus (modern Farsala, Thessaly, Greece) on August 9, 48 (see Lessons 64, "Mature the Enterprise," and 65, "Choose Quality over Quantity Every Time"). The defeated Pompey ignominiously deserted his troops at Pharsalus with Caesar in pursuit. Before Caesar caught up to him in Egypt, however, the young king Ptolemy XIII had Pompey assassinated and, aiming to curry favor with Caesar, sent him his severed head—at which (according to Caesar's early biographer Plutarch) the victor wept.

Veni, Vidi, Vici, and the Fatal Ides

Caesar spent the winter of 48–47 BCE in Alexandria, Egypt, where he sided with the fabled Queen Cleopatra against her brother-husband-coregent Ptolemy, whose forces Caesar defeated. Caesar and Cleopatra became two of history's most celebrated lovers, and she subsequently visited him more than once in Rome, where Caesar installed her in his villa just outside of the city even while he remained married to Calpurnia. It is believed that the couple had a son, Caesarion.

In 47, before returning to Rome from Egypt, Caesar fought and defeated Pharnaces, king of the Cimmerian Bosporus, who sought to regain the kingdom of Pontus, which had been lost to Rome by his father Mithradates. Caesar described the extraordinarily brief campaign in perhaps the most famous sentence ever penned in Latin: *"Veni, vidi, vici"*: "I came, I saw, I conquered." This victory won, he returned to Rome as absolute dictator (his term to elapse after a year), only to set off immediately for Africa to dispatch the diehard Pompeians who had rallied there. After defeating this force at Thapsus (its ruins still exist in Tunisia) in 46, he once again returned to Rome, was named dictator for ten years, but left the city in November to deal with Pompey's sons, who had fled to Spain.

His victory at the Battle of Munda (in modern Andalusia) on March 17, 45 BCE, definitively crushed the last Pompeian resistance, and he made his way back to Rome yet again, where he continued to introduce a host of political and cultural reforms (including the Julian calendar, which closely resembles the Gregorian calendar in use today) intended to reverse the long decline of Rome and the decay of the entire Greco-Roman world. Yet he was resolute in his refusal either to make himself emperor or to have kingship thrust upon him (see Lesson 46, "Know When to Be Caesar and Not to Be King").

We may count among Caesar's reforms his general clemency toward his many Roman enemies. At times ruthless—against the Gauls, sometimes capable of nothing less than genocide—Caesar was extravagantly liberal in granting amnesty to those in Rome who had opposed him for so long. He was anxious to avoid repeating the blood-soaked reign of Sulla, but so indiscriminate was Caesar's clemency that there was no end of foes available to conspire against him. They did just that, co-opting as well a number of his professed friends and partisans.

On the Ides of March—according to the Julian calendar, March 15—in the year 44 BCE, Caesar was accosted (as Plutarch tells it) upon his arrival outside the Senate by Tillius Cimber, who handed him a petition to recall an exiled brother. While Caesar was preoccupied in examining this, other conspirators crowded round, as if to voice support for the petition. As Caesar waved them away, Cimber suddenly pulled down Caesar's tunic from off of his shoulders.

"Ista quidem vis est!"—"This is violence!"—Caesar exclaimed.

Servilius Casca then thrust at Caesar's neck with his dagger. Exercising the reflexes of a warrior, the dictator turned, grabbed Casca by the arm, shouting "Casca, you villain, what are you doing?"

Terrified, Casca called out in Greek: "Help, brother!"

This cry brought all of the conspirators—some sixty men—into the action, among them Marcus Junius Brutus the Younger. An Optimate, he had long opposed Caesar, but after Caesar's victory over Pompey at the Battle of Pharsalus, he apologized and humbly sought Caesar's forgiveness and friendship. Both were eagerly granted, Caesar even appointing him governor of Gaul and, in 45 BCE, nominating him as urban praetor for the year 44. As the dagger blows fell—he was stabbed twenty-three times—Caesar's life swiftly bled away.

Suetonius recorded the report of some that Caesar's last words were spoken to Brutus in disbelief: *"Kai su, teknon?"*—"You too, child?" in English. Suetonius himself, however, claimed that Caesar had actually been silent in death. As for the modern world, the line it best remembers blends Latin with English: *"Et tu, Brute?"* ("And *you*, Brutus?"), followed by "Then fall, Caesar." Written by William Shakespeare some sixteen hundred years after the event, it is pure fiction.

Vision and Strategy

Lesson 1
Gamble/Invest

> "Caesar was gambling on his political future being bright and lucrative enough to cancel out his debts."
>
> ~ Adrian Goldsworthy, *Caesar: Life of a Colossus*

In 65 BCE, Julius Caesar was elected *aedile*, a magistrate whose responsibilities encompassed most of the practical tasks of running the city of Rome—everything from directing the upkeep of the great temples to ensuring that the city's sewers functioned properly. Beyond such quotidian tasks, the aedile was also responsible for organizing public festivals, games, and other entertainments. There were various public monies for these events, but Caesar, determined to impress, thrill, and delight the public beyond what any other aedile had ever achieved or could ever achieve, spent massive amounts of his personal funds to ensure that the ambitious spectacles he staged were runaway hits.

For this, he borrowed truly staggering sums. In his *Life of Caesar,* Plutarch calculated that, even before he officially entered office, Caesar was indebted to the tune of 1,300 talents, or 31 million sestertii. This was at a time when a Roman knight (a member of the equestrian order) was, by way of qualification for his station, required to hold property amounting to at least 400,000 sestertii. Thus young Caesar's debts amounted to nearly eighty times the wealth a nobleman of his time and place was required to possess.

To our modern sensibilities, buying public favor in this way seems to be an incredibly irresponsible gamble. In Caesar's day, it was not unusual—though the scope of his ambition and spending was nevertheless remarkable. What we would call a gamble, Caesar considered an investment. A Roman politician built his base of support through words, deeds, and cash translated into public works and public games.

> **From the beginning of** his political career, Caesar was willing to put skin in the game. As a military commander, he routinely laid his life on the line. As a rising politician, he mortgaged the present to stake a claim on the future. Do you share Caesar's nerve and Caesar's self-confidence?

■

Lesson 2
Look for a Way Around

"I would rather be in jail with Cato than here with you."
~Senator Marcus Petreius, to Consul Caesar,
in response to Caesar's ordering Cato to prison, 59 BCE

Julius Caesar was elevated to senior consul of Rome, a position of great power but brief duration. Within the single year allotted to his consulship, Caesar intended to breathe new life into the Roman Republic by rebalancing the relationship between the common people (whose interests were represented by populist politicians known as the Populares) and the patricians (whose party was known as the Optimates). In essence, Caesar proposed to bring about a bloodless revolution, lest Rome descend into an outright civil war between the people and patricians.

His first move was to introduce extensive land reform in order to give more Romans a real stake in the Roman state. At the time, the city of Rome was awash in dispossessed farmers and discharged legion veterans, none of whom had real work or a permanent place to live. Lawlessness, poverty, and general disorder increasingly came to characterize life in and around the capital. Caesar composed a bill that would relocate the urban dispossessed on state-held farms throughout all of Italy. Bowing to the patricians, Caesar proposed exempting from this redistribution the richest public lands of the Campania. His legislation also guaranteed that no one would be evicted from land legally held and that all current ownership would be recognized and upheld. Beyond this, a special land commission would be created to plan and execute a grand resettlement, which, Caesar argued, would bring urgently needed social and political stability to the Roman Republic.

The bill was so thoroughly thought out that when Caesar invited senators to raise objections to it, none were forthcoming. Nevertheless, a majority of the Senate was unwilling to alter a status quo that favored the Optimates. Unable to level any specific criticisms against the bill, they endeavored to delay passage of it, perhaps with the object of tabling it indefinitely. Cato (Marcus Porcius Cato Uticensis, known as Cato the Younger) rose to speak, delivering what today would be termed a *filibuster*, intended to run on until sunset, when the Senate, by law, would have to adjourn.

In an agony of frustration, Caesar cut him off. He ordered a lictor (a kind of sergeant at arms) to arrest Cato and take him off to prison. Predictably, this outraged the senatorial Optimates, who rose with the intent of following Cato into incarceration. Indeed, Caesar's uncharacteristic lapse of political self-restraint alienated even moderate senators, who likewise began to file out of the Senate. To one of them, Marcus Petreius, Caesar called out, demanding to know why he, a reasonable man, was leaving. His answer was devastating: "I would rather be in jail with Cato than here with you."

The senator's blunt declaration had two effects on Caesar. First, he immediately decided to cut his political losses by directly ordering Cato's release. To hold him, he realized, would only give his enemies a martyr around whom to rally. Second, and more importantly, Caesar resolved to waste no further time with the Senate. He would work around it, by appealing directly to the people of Rome. With that, he took the bill from the Senate and to the popular assembly, the Plebian Council.

> **Confronted by a wall** too high to climb and too hard to break through, look for a way around. Having found it, move along it.

■

Lesson 3
Provoke the Result You Want

> "You will not have your law this year–not even if all of you want it!"
> ~Junior Consul Marcus Calpurnius Bibulus, refusing before the
> Plebian Council to support Caesar's land reform bill of 59 BCE

Blocked by Senate patrician Optimates from passing a radical land reform bill, First Consul Julius Caesar appealed directly to the people through the Plebian Council (Lesson 2, "Look for a Way Around"). According to Roman law, the two consuls governed by consensus. Caesar therefore took along with him to the council the junior consul of Rome, Marcus Calpurnius Bibulus, who, he knew, was among those opposed to his bill. Before a cheering crowd–for land reform was seen as a great boon to the common people of Rome–Caesar asked Bibulus to present his arguments against the bill. Like the other Optimates, he had no specific criticisms to offer and objected to the bill only because it would bring change that undermined a status quo favorable to the patrician class. Embarrassed and befuddled, all Bibulus could muster was a mumbled announcement that he intended to allow no "innovations" this year.

Caesar then turned to the people, asking them to call on Bibulus to support the bill. "The law will pass, but only if he supports it," Caesar declared, referring to the consensus requirement. As Caesar hoped it would, this provoked Bibulus to an exclamation of mindless defiance. "You will not have your law this year," he shouted, as if speaking to children, then added: "not even if all of you want it!"

It was precisely the statement of tyranny—naked and arbitrary—Caesar had hoped to elicit. The indefensible public intransigence of Bibulus had given Caesar the anvil on which he forged an instant alliance with the people of Rome and their two most prominent and powerful champions, Pompey (Gnaeus Pompeius Magnus) and Crassus (Marcus Licinius Crassus). Caesar and these two men became that day the First Triumvirate, which would exert unofficial but very real ruling influence over Rome.

> **You can argue against** someone's bad idea, but it is far more effective to let the person himself expose his own idea in all its badness. If you would master the politics of power, emulate Caesar by provoking from your rivals precisely the result you want.

■

Lesson 4
Cultivate the Proactive Habit

> "The news was brought back to Caesar that the Helvetii were minded to march through the land of the Sequani and the Aedui into the borders of the Santones, which are not removed from the borders of the Tolosates, a state in the [Roman] Province. He perceived that this event would bring great danger upon the Province; for it would have a warlike tribe, unfriendly to the Roman people, as neighbours to a district which was at once unprotected and very rich in corn [cereal crops]. For these reasons he set Titus Labienus, lieutenant-general, in command of the fortification which he had made, and himself hurried by forced marches into Italy. There he enrolled two legions."
>
> ~Julius Caesar, *The Gallic War*, Book I

Untold generations of students of Latin have known well: *Gallia est omnis divisa in partes tres*—"All Gaul is divided into three parts." These opening words of Caesar's *The Gallic War,* his third-person account of his conquest of Gaul for the Roman Republic, describe the situation when he commenced military action in the region in 58 BCE. He was at the time proconsul and governor of Gallia Cisalpina (Cisalpine Gaul, roughly the territory of northern Italy), Provincia (the "Province," also known as Gallia Narbonensis or Gallia Transalpina [in English, Transalpine Gaul], located in what is now Languedoc and Provence, southern France), and Illyricum (encompassing parts of Albania, Croatia, and Bosnia and Herzegovina).

Some three and a half centuries before Caesar's arrival in Gaul, probably in 387 BCE (though tradition dates the event to 390), the Gauls defeated the army of the Roman Republic under Quintus Suplicius on the Allia River, not far from Rome. The capital was sacked and briefly besieged; only an epidemic among the Gauls added to a Roman tribute of a thousand pounds of gold prompted the conquerors to withdraw.

The invaders were gone, but the memory of the humiliation proved long indeed. The Battle of Allia was the beginning of an enduring Roman grudge against the Gallic and Celtic peoples. Over the centuries, as Rome extended its reach into their territories, the Republic concluded productive alliances and profitable trade relations with various tribes in Gaul; nevertheless, the Republic forgave neither the Gauls nor the Celts, and the motive of outright conquest was henceforth never very far from the Roman heart and mind.

At the time of Caesar's arrival in Gaul, Rome had a treaty of friendship with the Aedui, a tribe living in what is today the region of the Saône and Loire Rivers in France. In 58 BCE, Caesar received word that the Helvetii, a confederation of Celtic tribes occupying most of what is today Switzerland (even today, Switzerland is known formally as the "Confoederatio Helvetica"), were about to cross Roman-held Gallia Narbonensis to enter western France, where they planned to settle among a tribe known as the Santones.

Caesar knew the Helvetii as both warlike and highly skilled in warfare. He understood that if he, as a Roman commander, proved incapable of preventing an invasion that threatened both the Roman province as well as Rome's ally, the Aedui, the reputation, influence, authority, and power of Rome would be seriously diminished. He also decided that merely digging in and defending against the incursion of the Helvetii would be an insufficient response. What was required was an aggressive, proactive move. This would demonstrate not only Roman boldness and ferocity in combat, but also a thorough command of regional intelligence. By marching out to head off the Helvetii, Caesar would give the impression of a godlike omnipresence. Nothing is more powerful than being precisely where you are needed when you are needed.

For their part, the Helvetii prudently decided to avoid advancing directly through the Roman province; however, their alternative course lay through the land of the Aedui. That, as far as Caesar was concerned, was equally unacceptable. Commanding one of his generals to intercept the Helvetii, Caesar himself led legions from Italy as quickly as possible, by long-distance forced marches. Speed was the hallmark of a Caesarian military campaign. While other commanders sought to preserve their men's strength for combat, Caesar willingly invested it in the speed achieved by relentless marches. He who arrived first dictated the choice of battlefield and could generally occupy the all-important high ground. While long marches were exhausting, they ultimately saved lives and all but assured victory.

By the time the Helvetii reached the borderlands of the Allobroges, the Gallic tribe occupying the northern fringe of the Roman province, they were appalled to behold that Caesar had torn down the bridge of Geneva, thereby stopping them in their tracks. At this, the tribesmen sent a negotiating party to Caesar, promising to pass peacefully through the province. Caesar fully appreciated the toll the forced marches had taken on his men—for he had shared their hardship. To buy time for rest and recuperation as well as for the assembly of reinforcements and the fortification of the south bank of the Rhône, Caesar listened courteously to the Helvetian delegation, politely requested time to consider their proposal, set a date for his decision, and bid them return to their camp until that date. Believing they had won the day, the embassy agreed. By the time they returned, Caesar had, of course, built up his numbers and erected impressive fortifications. From this position of rest and strength, he issued his decision. It was a refusal to allow the tribe to cross the river.

Thwarted, the Helvetii did not offer battle, but instead embarked on the far more difficult northern route into Gaul via the territory of the Sequani (who appealed to Caesar for aid) and then laid waste to parts of the Aedui territory. Caesar attacked the Helvetii, whose numbers had been diminished by combat with the Sequani and Aedui, as they began crossing the Saône by boat, dealing them a hard defeat. He then rebuilt the bridge across the contested Saône, which encouraged the surviving Helvetii to send a new delegation to Caesar. The leader of this party, a man named Divico, offered to settle wherever Caesar dictated. Caesar responded by demanding hostages and ordering reparations to be made to the Aedui and Allobroges. When Divico insolently refused, alluding to a battle fought near Agendicum in 107 BCE, in which the Helvetii defeated a Roman army under Lucius Cassius Longinus, Caesar resolved to mount a major attack at Bibracte, near the modern town of Autun in Burgundy. The outcome of this battle, he believed, would not only eliminate the Helvetii as a threat, but would cement Roman control over the Aedui and the Sequani, thereby advancing the conquest of Gaul.

> **A reactive response** "deals with" a situation, whereas proactive movement and action *create* ownership of the situation. This is the difference between grappling with a problem and exploiting an opportunity. The risks of the proactive option are great, but the apparent safety of a reactive coping response, whether it is a defensive stance or a so-called strategic retreat, is an illusion. The reality is that both of these "coping" options are in fact self-inflicted losses.

Lesson 5
Complete Your Victory

> "Caesar dispatched letters and messages to the Lingones, ordering
> them not to give assistance by corn [cereal crops] or otherwise,
> and affirming that, if they gave such assistance, he would treat
> them in the same fashion as the Helvetii."
>
> ~Julius Caesar, *The Gallic War*, Book I

Although Caesar scored a decisive military victory against the
Helvetii at the Battle of Bibracte in 58 BCE, he noted that
approximately "130,000 persons survived the action, and marched
continuously the whole night." Exhausted by the desperate fight
and having taken time to bury their dead, his legions were unable
to pursue the survivors. By the time Caesar and his army were
ready to resume their march, the Helvetii had already reached the
borders of the Lingones, a Celtic tribe occupying the headwaters
of the Seine and Marne Rivers. Rather than press his forces in a
more desperate and debilitating pursuit, Caesar sent messages to
the Lingones, warning them not to succor the refugees on pain of
being forced to share their desperate straits. In this way, Caesar
completed his victory, extending his tactical win at Bibracte into a
full-scale strategic triumph. "The Helvetii," he wrote in *The Gallic
War*, "were compelled by lack of all provision to send deputies to
him to treat of surrender."

Caesar not only dictated uncompromising terms, he continued
to press his victory by ordering all neighboring tribes—thoroughly
intimidated by what his Roman legions had achieved—to hunt down
all remaining refugees and return them to his camp. These he
"treated . . . as enemies," whereas "all the remainder . . . he admitted
to surrender." On his command, they withdrew from Gaul to their
own borders, "whence they had started." He further ordered them
to "restore with their own hands the [Aeduan] towns and villages
which they had burnt." In return for the compliance of the defeated
Helvetii, Caesar ensured that they were adequately fed, ordering the

Allobroges (a Celtic tribe living between the Rhône and the Lake of Geneva, along what is today the Swiss-French border) to furnish them with an abundance of wheat and other cereal crops.

Create—and never relinquish—a comprehensive strategic vision by always extending tactical victory into strategic triumph. Follow through. Finish up. Push your gains. Strive for a total win and a permanent change in your favor. We think of giving up as something that is done only in defeat. Too often, however, it is the winner who gives up before perfecting the triumph of his enterprise. Gain, build, exploit, and prevail.

■

Lesson 6
Spot the Problem; Work the Problem

> "Perceiving that the Seventh Legion . . . was . . . harassed by the enemy, Caesar instructed the tribunes to close the legions gradually together, and then, wheeling, to advance against the enemy."
>
> ~Julius Caesar, *The Gallic War*, Book II

Caesar described the assault of the fearsome Belgic Nervii warriors at the Sabis River as a crisis in which he "had everything to do at one moment." He began by endeavoring to do just that, putting out numberless fires when and where they broke out. This, he knew, was necessary to keep his army from being utterly consumed, but it also prevented his organizing a concerted and effective counterattack. Gradually his multiple focus bought him a little time to begin building an increasingly potent defense against the attack and thereby, step by step, regain the initiative from the enemy.

The combat situation had to be engaged, on its own terms at the start; then, as openings presented themselves, the engagement could be increasingly aggressive. So, at first, Caesar allowed the situation to dictate his responses. He had no choice. His sole business during the early part of the battle was keeping his army alive and fighting. As the battle developed, however, he looked for intervals and places he might use to improve the situation, to get, as it were, a firm toehold in the combat. When he saw that his Seventh Legion was being badly mauled, he recognized both the problem and its solution. This recognition was his toehold. He put his foot in and prepared to regain the advantage against the attackers.

What he saw was that the Seventh was too isolated from the other legions that were just then starting to arrive from the rear lines. Because the enemy was between the Seventh and the arriving forces, Caesar could not simply order a closing of ranks. Instead, he directed his tribunes to "close the legions gradually together." This single direction concentrated precious energy, and once the legions were effectively united as a fighting force, Caesar gave the order to wheel—to turn about in a single disciplined formation—thereby shifting from a defensive stance to full attack mode.

In this great shift, timing was everything. Had he forced the legions together prematurely, there would have been slaughter as men bunched up in an uncoordinated fashion, too close to slash and thrust effectively. By bringing them together gradually, however, he gave his soldiers singular direction and purpose while also whittling away at the enemy. As soon as he perceived the attackers weaken, he ordered the all-out counterattack. As Caesar knew it would, this command both inspirited his men and gave them an even more intensively defined mission. The huddled fear and trembling chaos that accompany a desperate defense were replaced by a new order in which (Caesar wrote) "one soldier supported another." Now on the attack, what had been a frightened mob became an army once again, a team whose members had one another's backs. As a result, they no longer feared "that their rear would be surrounded by the enemy," and with this fear removed, "they began to resist more boldly and to fight more bravely." The very fact of enhanced performance further enhanced performance.

> **Nothing succeeds, they say,** like success. The time to fight the fear of failure is when you find yourself in the very process of failing. Struggle to attain and hold the clarity necessary to spot the problem, and then work the problem. *Any* problem will do. Make any material improvement in the situation, and you will begin to turn failure into success. *Any* success will do, as long as you seize it, amplify it, and build on it. Then offer it to your team as hard proof of *their* capacity for victory.

■

Lesson 7
Won the War? See to It You Don't Lose the Peace

"Caesar . . . bade them keep their own territory and towns, and commanded their neighbours to restrain themselves and their dependents from [committing] outrage and [giving] injury."
~Julius Caesar, *The Gallic War*, Book II

The fiercely fought Battle of the Sabis, in which skilled and committed Nervii warriors very nearly destroyed Caesar's army, ended instead by bringing (as Caesar wrote) "the name and nation of the Nervii almost to utter destruction." The survivors—the "older men, who . . . had been gathered with the women and children in the creeks and marshes"—abjectly surrendered to Caesar, expecting no mercy from him. They had caused great death and destruction. How, in defeat, could they expect anything but the same in return?

It was against what he knew to be their very expectation that Caesar now acted. Having won the war, he was determined not to lose the peace. "To show himself merciful towards their pitiful suppliance, Caesar was most careful for their preservation." Not only did he allow the remnant of the Nervii to retain their own territory and towns, he prevailed on neighboring tribes not to use their sadly depleted state as an excuse to prey upon and plunder them.

By this magnanimous policy, Caesar simultaneously demonstrated Roman invincibility and Roman maturity, justice, and mercy. Rome was thus exhibited as a terrible force to be feared as an enemy but as a generous source to be embraced as a friend—or as an enlightened conqueror.

Too many who engage in business see themselves as locked into a zero-sum game in which the existence of a winner necessitates the creation of a loser. Caesar believed that his victory did not require the total defeat of his enemy. To be sure, the victory achieved had to send a powerful and unmistakable message. It had to be unambiguous, but it did not require total annihilation.

Momentary victory may be raised to the level of enduring triumph through the judicious application of mercy as well as the violent application of destruction. In writing of the exploits of his father-in-law, General Gnaeus Julius Agricola, the Roman historian Tacitus (56–117 CE) quoted a defeated British chieftain on the subject of victory by the Roman legions: "where they make a desert, they call it peace." For Caesar in Gaul, such a definition of "victory" was hollow, unstable, and therefore totally unacceptable. The product of a scorched earth is desolation for victor and vanquished alike. Success is measured in creation, not ruin.

Lesson 8
Make It Happen

> "By what handiwork, said they, by what strength could men, especially of so puny a stature (for, as a rule, our stature, short by comparison with their own huge physique, is despised of the Gauls), hope to set so heavy a [siege] tower on [their stronghold] wall?"
>
> ~Julius Caesar, *The Gallic War*, Book II

After the Romans under Caesar defeated the mighty Nervii, most feared of the Belgic tribes, so decisively, the other tribes of Gaul either aligned themselves with Rome or withdrew from conflict—except for the Aduatuci, which Caesar described as a Germanic tribe originating in Jutland but dwelling by the first century BCE, like the Nervii themselves, in the eastern portion of the Belgae territory (the eastern part of modern Belgium) and descended from the formidable Cimbri, Teutones, and Ambrones tribes. The Aduatuci had been advancing to the aid of the Nervii until word of that people's devastation at the Battle of the Sabis persuaded the Aduatuci chieftains to abandon "all their towns and forts" and gather "all their stuff in one stronghold, which was admirably fortified by Nature" on what is today the Meuse River, upstream from the site of the Nervii defeat. Caesar described the Aduatuci town as looking "down over the steepest rocks" on every side of its circumference. On "one side only was left a gently sloping approach, not more than two hundred feet in breadth." This narrow approach the Aduatuci "had fortified with a double wall of great height" and were in the process of "setting stones of great weight and sharpened beams upon the wall" to make it even more impregnable.

Caesar set up camp nearby. The Aduatuci "made frequent sallies from the stronghold, and engaged in petty encounters with our troops." They dared not, however, emerge in large numbers from their fortress town for an all-out, showdown battle. Caesar responded to this situation with productive patience. He set about building around their entire stronghold (except for the side that abutted the Meuse River itself) his own "fortified rampart of fifteen thousand feet in circumference, with forts at close interval." This "circumvallation" (surrounding wall) in effect absorbed the enclosed fortress, completely cutting it off.

As Caesar's structure drew to completion, the Aduatuci remained holed up in their town, comforting themselves (according to Caesar) with the thought that the strength of mere men–especially Romans of puny stature compared with the "huge physique" of the Gauls–could never "hope to set so heavy a [siege] tower" against their wall. For such a tower was necessary for a besieger to effectively fire into a walled fortification.

Caesar did in fact order his engineers to build a colossal siege tower, the purpose of which was to provide covered platforms from which his archers and ballista men–operating massive "ballista" catapults–could fire their missiles over the fortress walls. What the Aduatuci had not counted on was the mobility of the great tower. This tower was mounted on wheels and, through the combined strength of men and animals, would be rolled up the ramp Caesar built, to a position near the town walls. In fact, Caesar never even had to begin actual bombardment from his tower. The mere sight of the great structure in motion terrified the Aduatuci, who had never before seen so "novel and extraordinary" a sight. In response, they immediately "sent deputies to Caesar to treat of peace." The emissaries explained their supposition "that the Romans did not wage war without divine aid, inasmuch as they could move forward at so great a speed engines of so great a height." This being the case, "they therefore submitted themselves and all they had to the power of Rome."

Obstacles, whatever their origin—natural or human—can be regarded as either game-ending or game-on. If you are resigned to (or satisfied with) the status quo, you will define certain obstacles as immutable and absolute boundaries to the activity of your enterprise. If, however, you believe an endeavor needs to strive, develop, and grow, a given obstacle may be a game changer, but never a game ender.

Caesar treated the formidable obstacle of a town amply fortified by both nature and man as a challenge and an opportunity. It was a challenge to overcome, but he understood that overcoming it presented an opportunity to overawe the enemy and thereby achieve absolute victory. The difference between yielding to opposition and overcoming it is the difference between accepting prevailing circumstances as they are and looking upon prevailing circumstances as something that can be favorably changed. The second attitude requires the will and the means to make favorable circumstances happen.

■

Lesson 9
A Definition of Victory

> "And for those achievements, upon receipt of Caesar's despatches,
> a fifteen days' thanksgiving was decreed, an honour that had
> previously fallen to no man."
>
> ~Julius Caesar, *The Gallic War*, Book II

The index and evaluation of victory may be subject to more than a single measure: territory acquired, sovereignty changing hands, an enemy diminished or destroyed, stability secured, conquest made or conquest defeated, people enslaved or people liberated. For a leader, however, one measure, one index, is more crucial and more certain than any other: A victory builds, magnifies, and broadcasts reputation.

Caesar's achievements in Gaul during the years 58 and 57 BCE, the first phase of the Gallic War, generated (he wrote) "so mighty a report" throughout Gaul and the Germanic peoples east of the Rhine that all were prepared to do his bidding; even the warlike and purportedly intractable Germans promised "that they would give hostages and do [Caesar's] commands."

A "mighty report"—the formidable reputation of Roman arms— pacified Gaul and its neighbors to the east (for the time being, at least), and, returning to Italy preceded by his dispatches from the front, Caesar found himself the object of an unprecedented Roman thanksgiving. The personal reputation he created by his victories in Gaul, which both expanded and stabilized the foreign empire of the Roman Republic, laid the foundation for a subsequent rise to power as unprecedented as the more immediate acts of thanksgiving.

Success in business is most often measured by the bottom line. Inasmuch as money is the language of business, this measure cannot be denied or even argued with, any more than one can argue with the final numerical score of a competitive game, whether football or table tennis.

Yet no one would say that a high score is the sole value of winning.

Victory creates the more enduring value of reputation, which is a force that drives repeated and continued success. If victory raises an enterprise, reputation sustains it. Caesar grasped this principle throughout all of his military campaigns. The Roman Empire was built in part on his conquests and in even larger part on the reputation he created by those conquests. Likewise, your own record of achievement may build business for your organization, but unless it simultaneously builds your personal reputation and, with it, the reputation of your enterprise, your success will never be more than partial and attenuated. Creating a "mighty report" is the difference between the situation of a competent salesman, who is content to make this or that sale, and a truly consummate salesman, whose objective is not merely to make a sale, but to create one customer after another, each one a source of repeated and continued business. Reputation is leverage, and leverage is finally the most enduring definition of victory.

■

Lesson 10
Nurture What You Need

> "The Suebi are by far the largest and most warlike nation among the Germans."
>
> ~Julius Caesar, *The Gallic War*, Book IV

Caesar already professed genuine respect for his most formidable enemies, paramount among whom were the Suebi, sometimes called the Suevi, who lived in the Rhine region of what is today Germany and repeatedly invaded or threatened to invade Gaul. In calling them the "most warlike nation among the Germans," Caesar was not content merely to state a fact. With his customary analytical thoroughness, he sought to discover the sources of their prowess. He investigated thoroughly and concluded that one source was their strict alternation of the roles of stay-at-home farmer and conquering warrior. Every year, a thousand warriors set out on campaigns beyond the Suebi borders while the rest of the men stayed at home to work the farms. The next year, the warriors would return home to take up farming and the farmers would leave to fight. "By this means neither husbandry nor the theory and practice of war is interrupted," Caesar admiringly explained.

Caesar marveled at a society that had set itself up for the continuous, uninterrupted application of warfare. So that those who farmed for a year did not become permanently attached to home life and land, he observed, the Suebi "have no private or separate holding of land, nor are they allowed to abide longer than a year in one place for their habitation." The Suebi, Caesar came to understand, did not merely arrange their political and economic system to facilitate war, they bred up a race of warriors, literally nurturing them. "They make not much use of corn [cereal crops] for food, but chiefly of milk and of cattle, and are much engaged in hunting; and this, owing to the nature of the food, the regular exercise, and the freedom of life—for from boyhood up they are not schooled in a sense of duty or discipline, and do nothing whatever against their wish—nurses their strength and makes men of immense bodily stature." They also "have regularly trained themselves to wear nothing, even in the coldest localities, except skins, the scantiness of which leaves a great part of the body bare, and they bathe in the rivers. They give access to traders rather to secure purchasers for what they have captured in war than to satisfy any craving for imports. . . . They suffer no importation of wine whatever, believing that men are thereby rendered soft and womanish for the endurance of hardship."

There is a single essential difference between the Caesars of the world and the rest of the planet's inhabitants. The mass of humanity accepts the world into which it is born. The Caesars, in contrast, resolve to change it to better suit themselves. To them, reality is a lump awaiting shape. Nature demands nurture, according to the Caesars. If this Caesarean vision can build warriors, so it can create entrepreneurs and those who lead them.

■

Lesson 11
Leave No Enemy Behind

> "He did not wish to leave an enemy in his rear."
>
> ~Julius Caesar, *The Gallic War*, Book IV

The Morini were a tribe of the Belgae, who lived in what is today the region around Boulogne and Calais, France. As Caesar prepared to embark on his first expedition to the island of Britain, he was approached by emissaries from the Morini, who tendered their amends for previous attacks against the Romans and made a promise that they would henceforth do as Caesar commanded.

"Caesar thought this overture exceedingly opportune," yet it was not his practice to allow pleasing promises and welcome news to lull him into the complacency of wishful thinking. Both the "lateness of the season"—winter was rapidly approaching—and his unwillingness to delay his departure for Britain argued against his making any military demonstration to impress the Morini; nevertheless, he was determined not to violate a cardinal rule for any military commander: leave no enemy or potential enemy behind.

The rear of an advancing force is always vulnerable to attack, and lines of supply and communication, vital to any army, must also be protected from disruption. Something had to be done in this situation, and Caesar "therefore ordered them to furnish a large number of hostages," which he held to guarantee the good behavior of the Morini while he was in Britain.

"Watch your back" may be a cliché, but it is also an indispensable leadership policy. Human beings have two forward-facing eyes. They are equipped by nature to look ahead rather than behind. This forward focus is crucial to progress, but it is insufficient for survival. Like a military campaign, business must be conducted in multiple dimensions and from all directions. Just because you may enjoy the exhilarating momentum of a bold and rapid advance, make certain you leave no rival or potential rival behind, unseen, unmonitored, and uncontrolled. A majority of military historians have criticized Caesar as overeager to advance into Britain. Yet even they must acknowledge the attention he devoted to the Morini at his back.

■

Lesson 12
Master PSYOPS

"All these proceedings tempted the enemy to lead their forces . . .
to form line on unfavourable ground."
~Julius Caesar, *The Gallic War*, Book V

Julius Caesar was a master of the art of deception. Far from being a tactical adjunct to combat, deception is at the very heart of warfare. Deception is vital because it is a means of creating the reality you want your enemy to see and on which you want him to base his tactics and his actions–to *your* advantage. Modern practitioners of the military art call deception PSYOPS, "psychological operations," a branch of warfare that (in the language of the U.S. Joint Chiefs of Staff during World War II) "employs *any* weapon to influence the mind of the enemy."

During Caesar's campaign against the fierce Nervii tribe in Gaul, Caesar was on the march to rescue Quintus Cicero and his legion, which lay under perilous siege. While en route and camped for the night, Caesar received word that the Nervii had suddenly lifted their siege and were now forming up to turn on Caesar's own approaching forces.

For his part, Caesar was so eager to engage the enemy that he broke camp at first light. He had not advanced very far when he caught sight of the Nervii. It was immediately apparent that they significantly outnumbered his force, and, even worse, they occupied an advantageous high-ground position. A courageous but conventional commander might have resigned himself to fighting with what resources he had and on what ground the enemy occupied, trusting to fortune or the gods for a favorable outcome. Caesar, however, was far from being a conventional commander. "It was a very dangerous thing for so slender a force to fight on unfavourable ground," he wrote. Besides, now that Cicero was no longer besieged and in danger, there was no pressing need for haste. Caesar "halted, therefore, and proceeded to entrench his camp in the most favourable position to be found; and small as was the camp itself, as it was for scarce seven thousand men, and those, too, without baggage, he nevertheless compressed it by narrowing the streets [roadways within the camp] as much as possible, with the object of incurring the utmost contempt on the part of the enemy." In short, Caesar *wanted* the Nervii to believe his force was pitiably small, inadequate, and poorly supplied: a sitting duck.

"Petty encounters of cavalry took place" during the day, Caesar recorded. He made attempts to determine "if by pretending fear he could draw the enemy" from its favorable ground to "his own ground, and fight on this side of the valley, in front of the camp." His object was to begin the battle by compelling the enemy to surrender its greatest advantage, the advantage of a favorable position, before a single major blow had been exchanged. In the meantime, "Caesar purposely ordered the cavalry to give way [in its skirmishes] and to retire into camp," as if terrified. Simultaneously, he "ordered the camp to be fortified with a higher rampart on all sides, the gates to be barricaded, and as much confusion and pretence of fear as possible to be shown in the execution of these arrangements."

At length, the carefully orchestrated deception succeeded. "All these proceedings tempted the enemy to lead their forces across [from their side of the valley to Caesar's side] and to form line on [what was to them] unfavourable ground." Now it was the Nervii who were ripe for plucking. Caesar gave the order, and his men burst out of camp with a speed and ferocity that stunned and overwhelmed the over-confident Nervii. In panic, they ran. They were so "speedily [put] to flight," Caesar wrote, "that never a man stood to fight." Because of this, Caesar "slew a great number of them and stripped all of their arms."

Decline to accept "unfavorable ground" just because that is what happens to lie before you. Instead, manage your rival's perception to allow you to claim a more advantageous reality. Use "*any* weapon to influence the mind" of those against whom you must compete for the favorable ground. The author of the ever-popular *The Art of War*, Sun Tzu, was an ancient Chinese general who lived some five hundred years before Julius Caesar and was certainly unknown to the Romans. Yet Sun Tzu's famous assertion—"Every battle is won before it is even fought"—is a sentence that might just as well have been uttered by Caesar himself. It is the foundation of all truly successful strategy.

■

Lesson 13
Winner Take Nothing

> "Only, the Gauls must consent to destroy with their own hands
> their corn-supplies and burn their buildings, seeing that by such
> loss of property they were acquiring dominion and liberty for
> all time."
>
> ~Julius Caesar, *The Gallic War*, Book VII

At a grand council of Gallic tribes held at Bibracte (near modern Autun in Burgundy, France), Vercingetorix, chieftain of the Averni (a Gallic tribe living in what is today the French Auvergne), was popularly acclaimed supreme commander of all the Gallic rebels against Rome.

He was a formidable choice. A military leader of great ability and intelligence, Vercingetorix reasoned that, as an invading force, the Romans were burdened by a great disadvantage in that, operating far from their homeland, they had to depend on local sources of supply. He therefore proposed avoiding all-or-nothing pitched battles—for Caesar, his generals, and his legions were, of course, extraordinarily able warriors—and instead advocated exploiting the inherent weakness of the invaders' situation by waging a war of attrition and starvation. To succeed in this strategy, Vercingetorix warned, would require absolute and unbroken adherence to a strict and universal scorched-earth policy. All of the tribal leaders and their people had to agree to "destroy with their own hands their corn-supplies [cereal crops] and burn their buildings" in order to deprive the Romans of all local sources of sustenance and succor. Hunger, not combat, would, in the fullness of time, destroy Caesar and his army.

It was a reasonable strategy, but, in the end, the Gauls could not be moved to thoroughly pursue a policy, which, while certainly destructive to Caesar and his legions, was by definition also self-defeating. If the Romans were hungry, so were the Gauls.

For his part, Caesar marveled at the willingness of Vercingetorix even to attempt such a strategy, by which the equation of victory versus defeat was utterly flattened into a proposition whereby the winner, gaining nothing, was made equal to the loser.

Of all the enemy commanders Caesar faced, none was more formidable than Vercingetorix, and while he was a fierce and able general, who ably wielded very large forces, what Caesar found most difficult to combat was his willingness to change the very basis of war by an act of collective self-sacrifice.

Advanced business thinkers look for ways to convert zero-sum competition, in which one side must lose for the other to win, into collaborative, synergistic scenarios in which competitors can benefit mutually and to a greater degree than either could separately in a conventional win-or-lose situation. The ultimate problem in adhering to the zero-sum formula is that the fear of defeat may tempt the use of scorched-earth tactics in which both sides lose. Caesar was certainly capable of great cruelty, even to the point of genocide. Yet he far preferred (as he often declared) resorting to "policy instead of the sword." In this spirit, he made productive alliances with far more Gallic tribes than he defeated, let alone annihilated, in war.

■

Lesson 14

Victory for the Sake of Victory Is No Triumph

"He was led to object to a pitched battle [because] even if the enemy were driven to flight, a victory could not greatly promote his final success."

~Julius Caesar, *Civil Wars*, Book I

The Battle of Ilerda (modern Lleida, Spain) was fought from June through much of August 49 BCE, during Caesar's civil war against the Optimates, as the forces loyal to the Senate and to Pompey the Great (Gnaeus Pompeius Magnus) were known. The long battle consisted mostly of maneuver rather than large-scale combat because Caesar deliberately and repeatedly avoided a pitched battle with the enemy army. Instead of forcing a costly showdown fight, he compelled the Pompeian army to move from one disadvantageous position into another, even more precarious, until he eventually blockaded the enemy army "in every way," so that "their baggage animals were soon "without fodder" and the men themselves were in dire "want of water, firewood, and forage." Cut off and desperate, the enemy "beg[ged] for a conference." In response to their pleas, Caesar compelled them to "come to a place which [he] chose." In this way, almost without bloodshed, the Pompeian armies of the legates (generals) Afranius and Petreius were defeated and surrendered to Caesar.

Had Caesar instead earlier yielded to his own troops' agitation for a "pitched battle," he believed that, even in victory, he would have lost the opportunity to completely neutralize the enemy forces. As Caesar explained in his account of the battle, "the propinquity [nearness] of the camps [his camp and that of the Pompeians] afforded the conquered a speedy retreat in their flight." In other words, the defeated enemy would likely have gotten away and thereby lived to fight another day. Avoiding an all-out battle was clearly the best option, but it was also the most difficult to choose, since "to appear to have shunned a battle against the general sentiment of the troops, and his credit in the eyes of the world, involved serious detriment to [Caesar's] cause." Great maturity of judgment and a strong will were required to make and to carry out the decision to withhold battle.

As a military leader, Caesar valued victory. As a military leader with broader political ambitions, however, he did not worship it. He understood victory to be a means to a larger end and, therefore, that victory for its own sake would be no triumph.

Entrepreneurs and executives are typically aggressive, competitive "type A" individuals. Facts of business life, these personality and attitude orientations can be key drivers of success, but they can just as easily prompt a leader to look upon winning as an end in itself. A leader's capacity to recognize that victory in any particular exchange, transaction, or deal is a means and not an end is a hallmark of mature judgment.

■

Lesson 15
Choose the Hardest Way

> "They were caught off their guard, for they thought themselves fortified by the Cevennes [Mountains] as by a wall, and not even a solitary traveller had ever found the paths open at that [winter] season."
>
> ~Julius Caesar, *The Gallic War*, Book VII

The Arverni were a Gallic tribe whose territory was what is now the Auvergne in the south of France. It is a region bounded on the southwest by the Cevennes Mountains, which were considered totally impassable during the season of heavy winter snows. In 52 BCE, the winter was exceptionally brutal, with snows (according to Caesar) blocking the mountain passes to a depth of six feet.

Who would even think of marching an army through the Cevennes in a season of snows that were taller than a man?

Caesar ordered his men to clear away the six-foot-deep snow, a labor requiring what he himself described as "a supreme effort of the troops." It was a task so unthinkably hard that the enemy, believing it impossible, refused to think about it and therefore left themselves vulnerable to an "impossible" attack.

"Caesar commanded the cavalry to extend on as broad a front and strike as much terror into the enemy as possible." And, under the chieftain Vercingetorix, the fiercest and most skillful of all the Gallic commanders who ever went up against Caesar, the Arverni were a most formidable enemy. Nevertheless, the sudden appearance of the Roman legions before their eyes created widespread panic among them. No tactic, no weapon, no military force is more powerful or more effective than actually achieving the apparently impossible.

> **Sometimes the best,** most rewarding, course of action is the very hardest. Embrace what others deem impossible, find a way to achieve it, create panic among your competitors. Easy may cost little, but it rarely pays big.

■

Lesson 16
View from the Top

> "Now that I am the greatest man in Rome, it will be more difficult to push me down to second place than it would be to push a second-rank man to the bottom."
>
> ~Julius Caesar, quoted in Suetonius, *The Twelve Caesars*

Caesar set out to conquer Gaul in order to enlarge the empire of the Roman Republic and to transform the very face of the world. He also had a more personal motive. By fashioning himself into the greatest conqueror the Republic had ever known, he would become the "greatest man in Rome." This, he believed, would make him difficult to overthrow. For in Caesar's view, it was the ranks below the uppermost that were subject to the bitterest squabbling and most vulnerable to political instability. As any general knows, the safest and most advantageous position is on the highest ground.

Conventional people will tell you that it is lonely at the top. This is a feeling they can only imagine, of course, because they have never actually reached the top—nor do they wish to. Conventional people prefer the middle levels, the anonymity of which seems to promise safety and security. Unconventional people, the kind of people who become leaders, recognize that the strongest place to be is at the top of any enterprise. Here is where you have the most commanding view and can see whatever may come your way.

■

Lesson 17
Make Your Vision Big but Its Execution Even Bigger

"Under the command of Caius Caesar, we have fought a war inside Gaul; in the past we have merely repelled attacks. . . . I see that Caius Caesar's thinking has been very different. For he did not feel it sufficient to fight only against those already in arms against the Roman people, but felt that all of Gaul should be brought under our dominion. Therefore he has, with stunning good fortune, smashed in battle the greatest and fiercest tribes of Germans and Helvetii, and terrified the other peoples, checked them and brought under our domination and power of the Roman people; our general, our soldiers, and the arms of the Roman people have now made their way through regions and nations which till now have not even been known by story or written account."

~Cicero, speech to the Senate, 56 BCE, translated in Adrian

Goldsworthy's, *Caesar: Life of a Colossus*

Caesar and the great orator, philosopher, and statesman Marcus Tullius Cicero were often fierce rivals, but as Cicero's speech to the Senate in 56 BCE describing Caesar's campaigns in Gaul demonstrates, he thoroughly admired Caesar's vision and strategy in that vast region.

Caesar's realized intention was, as Cicero explained, to do what no Roman general had ever even thought of doing before: to not merely respond to Gallic aggression, but to preempt it utterly by extending the reach of Rome into the farthest corners of Gaul. Cicero fully appreciated the original, audacious, out-of-the-box thinking that Caesar's vision of war represented. It was to fight a war for the purpose of achieving permanent change—in the case of Gaul, nothing less than an enduring alteration of the known world. The vision was at once proactive, preemptive, and thorough, the elevation of local and regional tactics to the level of grand global strategy.

Caesar was not satisfied with war as it was conventionally fought in his time. Campaigns were routinely undertaken in response to some threat and with the limited objective of checking that threat. This, Caesar recognized, doomed states to fight an endless series of conflicts, to put out this or that brushfire without ever discovering the source of the conflagration and quenching it forever.

In Gaul, Caesar encountered a bewildering array of tribes and peoples, some of whom had attacked Roman interests, some of whom had not. He resolved not to discriminate among the tribes, not to treat Gaul as a collection of groups to be individually and selectively repelled only when they became aggressive. Instead, he regarded it as one vast region and one enormous population ripe for conquest once and for all time. His vision was to fight a war in Gaul that would end the necessity of future wars in Gaul.

Caesar's ultimate ambition was not merely to rule Rome, but to alter the contours of the world on a scale unprecedented both in its geopolitical and its temporal dimensions. He envisioned an empire not only great in lands and peoples but destined to endure through all time. This drove him to conduct military campaigns of unprecedented scope. If conquest was the job of empire, his intention was to finish the job.

Any genuinely enterprising vision must balance immediate tactical needs with long-term strategy. The key to building a truly enduring enterprise, however, is to put your thumb on the side of the scales that lean toward the future. Emulate Caesar in Gaul: Make your vision big but its execution even bigger.

■

Lesson 18
Examine Your Motives

"[In Gaul, Caesar] had taken by storm more than 800 towns, subdued 300 nations, and of three million men, who made up the total of those with whom at different times he fought pitched battles, he had killed one million of them in hand-to-hand fighting and took many more prisoners, with more than one million being sold into slavery."

~ Plutarch, *Life of Caesar*

If Plutarch's summary of eight years of warfare in Gaul is accurate, out of three million combatants, Caesar killed or captured more than two-thirds. Modern scholars believe that the total population of Gaul was about twelve million, which means that Caesar was responsible for killing or capturing more than 10 percent of the region's people. While troop numbers and casualty figures from ancient warfare are generally considered to be grossly inflated, there is no question that the campaigns of the Gallic War were extraordinarily costly. Indeed, Caesar's contemporaries regarded their cost, scope, and gains as unprecedented.

The devastation of Gaul won an empire for Rome and great power for Julius Caesar. Even so, both history and many of Caesar's contemporaries and near contemporaries have questioned his motives. Most notably, Seneca (54 BCE–ca. 39 CE), the famed rhetorician and writer, believed that Caesar pursued nothing but "glory."

It is a word that does not sound well in modern ears. To kill and enslave so many for the sake of "mere" glory seems manifestly an obscenity, and many of us would have no trouble condemning Caesar for such a motive. Yet if Caesar could again put on mortality and allow us to confront him, he would likely not deny having sought glory and having killed so many to obtain it. For whatever else Caesar was, he was a man who knew precisely what he was about. He understood his driving motive, and it was a motive perfectly suited to his time and place. No commodity was more valuable in the ancient Roman world than glory. It was the currency of politics, wealth, power, and empire. To achieve glory was to possess a force with which one could recruit armies, command loyalty, and win over entire peoples. For us, the question of whether a lust for glory is worth the sacrifice of untold lives is simple to answer: *No, it is not worth it.* For Caesar and most, though not all, of his contemporaries, the answer was equally obvious: *Yes, it is worth any cost.*

Examine your purpose, your ambitions, and your aspirations. Evaluate them in terms of ethics, immediate tactics, long-term strategy, risk and reward, the bottom line, and the enduring as well as evolving identity both of yourself and your organization. Be certain you fully understand, value, and embrace your motives in all of these dimensions. Only when you are fully confident of that understanding, prepare yourself to meet, answer, and if necessary to resist and refute the objections, pressures, distortions, and motives of others. In this way, you create the identity of a leader.

2

Decision and Action

Lesson 19
Temper Policy with Pragmatism

> "The problem is that people only remember what happens last. Thoughtless men will consider not the evil deeds these criminals have committed but instead the punishment they have received from us—if that punishment is unusually harsh."
>
> ~Julius Caesar, appeal to the Senate for clemency for the
> Catiline conspirators, 63 BCE

Lucius Sergius Catilina, known to history as Catiline, was a debt-burdened patrician who, with a group of men in similar straits, conspired against the Roman Republic. Thwarted in his desperate attempt to achieve election as consul and charged with malfeasance as governor of Rome's African province, Catiline assembled a cadre of disgruntled senators and equestrians (knights) along with a handful of Etruscans and set about raising an army with the intention of commencing a civil war that would bring him to power. On the night of October 18, 63 BCE, however, Marcus Licinius Crassus brought letters to Marcus Tullius Cicero, at the time consul of Rome. The letters warned of what historians now call the Catiline Conspiracy.

On the very next day, October 19, Cicero read the letters to the Senate, which responded by giving Cicero absolute dictatorial power and by imposing on Rome a state of martial law. Just as this occurred, news reached Rome of a mass slave revolt in southern Italy. Amid a general panic in the capital, the Senate ordered an army to be raised. In the meantime, Catiline's confederates actively agitated and fostered the rebellion, and on November 6, Catiline himself boldly announced that he was leaving the city of Rome to take personal command of the revolt. Cicero responded with spectacular orations condemning Catiline, who, in turn, retaliated by stirring popular opposition to the aristocratic Cicero. Catiline also planned acts of arson throughout Rome as well as the assassination of Cicero.

While the conspiracy roiled in southern Italy and in Rome, Catiline's confederates made an offer of alliance to the Allobroges, a Celtic tribe living in Gaul between what today are the Rhône River and the Lake of Geneva. In so doing, however, the conspirators had finally overplayed their hand. Unwilling to suffer the wrath of Rome, the Allobroges reported the traitorous proposal, which was in turn conveyed to Cicero. Telling the Allobroges to pretend to join the conspiracy, Cicero orchestrated an ambush of some of the principal conspirators at Rome's Milvian Bridge. Captured, they were held by authority of the Senate.

Cicero eloquently urged his fellow senators to authorize the immediate execution—without trial—of the conspirators. Caesar, who certainly condemned the conspiracy, nevertheless argued for clemency on the grounds that the common people were already at odds with the Senate and the patricians, and that although the overwhelming majority of the people patriotically deplored Catiline's attack on Rome, they would interpret the summary execution of the conspirators not as an act of justice but of vengeance—the vengeance of the aristocracy against the people. While there was no question, Caesar argued, that the conspirators, according to the principles of justice, deserved to die, a decision for clemency was far more pragmatic because, "Thoughtless men will consider not the evil deeds these criminals have committed but instead the punishment they have received from us—if that punishment is unusually harsh."

Despite Caesar's arguments, Cicero prevailed, and the conspirators were executed, without trial, in December 63 BCE. The Senate immediately honored Cicero with the high title of "Pater Patriae"—Father of His Country—and launched an assault on Catiline, killing him and ending the conspiracy. Events of the longer term proved the utility of Caesar's pragmatism, however. In 58 BCE, Publius Clodius Pulcher, tribune of the plebs and a personal and political enemy of Cicero, introduced in the Senate the *Leges Clodiae*, which outlawed, on pain of exile, the execution of any Roman citizen without a trial. The legislation was applied ex post facto to Cicero, who had executed the Catiline conspirators four years earlier, and although Cicero cogently defended himself—reasonably claiming that the emergency dictatorial powers the Senate had given him made him immune to prosecution and punishment—he could find no support from senators and consuls, who were now unwilling to alienate the common citizens of Rome. Cicero therefore went into exile. Although he returned on August 5, 57 BCE, he never regained his former political power.

Upholding any principle as "absolute" should never be an excuse for unthinking action. There is no viable method of automating leadership. Exercise individual and specific judgment in all matters and at all times. Be prepared to temper policy with pragmatism.

■

Lesson 20
Reject Provocation as a Motive to Action

"The Helvetii . . . began . . . to provoke the Romans to a fight. Caesar kept his troops from fighting, accounting it sufficient for the present to prevent the enemy from plundering, foraging, and devastation."

~Julius Caesar, *The Gallic War*, Book I

After the Helvetian envoy Divico refused Caesar's demand for hostages following the defeat of the Helvetii at the Battle of the Saône (in what is today eastern France), the Helvetii cavalry routed a small portion of the Roman army. This emboldened them to take a stand and goad Caesar's legions into a fight on ground favorable to the Helvetii and unfavorable to the Romans. With his men yearning for instant vengeance, Caesar ordered restraint. He had four reasons. First, he never wanted to fight on ground dictated by the enemy. To do so was to surrender even before a single blow was landed. Combat should be on ground of one's own choosing and always to one's tactical advantage. Second, it was sufficient in the short run merely to demonstrate to his allies, the Aedui tribe, that the Romans could prevent the Helvetii from plundering and devastating their country. Moreover, preventing this also kept the Helvetii from foraging to feed themselves and their animals. Finally, by avoiding a fight now, Caesar preserved the option to find, occupy, and fortify superior ground for a subsequent battle—which he would do shortly, at Bibracte, near what is today Autun in Burgundy, France.

Impulse is the enemy of strategy and tactics. Although it is important to exploit passion and zeal, managing these is even more critical. Like any other source of energy, emotion can be frittered away, wasted, expended destructively, or it can be conserved, shaped, and directed productively. Caesar possessed the tactical and strategic vision to understand when such self-control was warranted, and he further commanded the credibility to enforce his self-control on those he led.

■

Lesson 21
Value Only Reliable Information, Then Get It

> "As [Caesar] would not have those matters threshed out in presence of a company, he speedily dismissed the meeting. . . . Liscus now spoke with greater freedom and boldness."
>
> ~Julius Caesar, *The Gallic War*, Book I

Engaged in war with the fierce Helvetii tribe, which had invaded Gaul, Caesar desperately needed to maintain the subordinate alliance of Rome's tributary tribe, the Aedui. When he received intelligence from an Aeduan chief named Liscus that a revolt was brewing against Roman authority, Caesar listened—up to a point. He believed that Dumnorix, brother of another powerful Aeduan leader, Diviciacus, and rival of Liscus, "was indicated in these remarks of Liscus." Instead of yielding to what must have been his anxious impulse to hear more right away, Caesar called a halt to the conversation and sent everyone away, except for Liscus. He then "questioned him separately on his statement in the assembly." In the absence of the others, Liscus spoke, as Caesar hoped and expected he would, "with greater freedom and boldness," revealing in detail the treachery of Dumnorix. With this "free" revelation in hand, Caesar next sought corroboration by questioning "others privately upon the same matters." In this way, he confirmed the intelligence and ascertained the full extent of Dumnorix's plans as well as his motives and acts of treachery already committed, including the fact that Dumnorix had led the Helvetii through the borders of the Sequani against Caesar's orders.

"Caesar deemed all this to be cause enough for him either to punish Dumnorix himself, or to command the state to do so."

In any enterprise, information flows through many portals, some public, some private, some official, some under the table or over the transom, some digital, and some face-to-face. Few managers suffer from a dearth of information; however, *reliable* information is always precious and, too often, in critically short supply. No one understood this more clearly than Julius Caesar, who exercised the utmost discretion in order to extract from the prodigal flood of information the precious trickle of truly reliable, useful—"actionable"—information. It was only upon this carefully defined and painstaking obtained species of data that he based his decisions and actions.

■

Lesson 22

Anticipate Consequences, Then Manage Them Proactively

"Caesar deemed all this to be cause enough for him either to punish Dumnorix himself, or to command the state to do so. To all such procedure there was one objection."

~Julius Caesar, *The Gallic War*, Book I

After Caesar secured irrefutable evidence that the Aeduan tribal chief Dumnorix was only pretending to be his ally, was in reality plotting a revolt against Rome, and had already committed treachery (Lesson 21, "Value Only Reliable Information, Then Get It"), he concluded that some harsh sanction must be applied. Yet, even now, in the face of overwhelming evidence, Caesar resisted the impulse to immediate action. Instead, he himself raised "one objection" against inflicting punishment, namely "the knowledge that Diviciacus, the brother of Dumnorix, showed the utmost zeal for the Roman people, the utmost good will towards himself [that is, toward Caesar], in loyalty, in justice, in prudence alike remarkable"; Caesar feared that punishing Dumnorix "might offend" Diviciacus. For this reason, before acting on what now seemed certain evidence of treachery, Caesar summoned Diviciacus to his quarters.

As he had earlier arranged to speak privately with Liscus, who informed against Dumnorix, Caesar now sent his regular coterie of interpreters away and summoned instead Gaius Valerius Procillus, "a leading man in the Province of Gaul and his own intimate friend, in whom he had the utmost confidence upon all matters." Valerius and Valerius alone would be his interpreter in this most critical matter. Through him, Caesar laid the case before Diviciacus. In response, the Aeduan leader embraced Caesar and through tears beseeched him "not to pass too severe a judgment upon his brother." Grateful of Caesar's show of empathy and respect, Diviciacus opened up to him frankly and completely:

> I know that the reports are true, and no one is more pained thereat than I, for at a time when I had very great influence in my own state and in the rest of Gaul, and he [Dumnorix] very little, by reason of his youth, he owed his rise to me; and now he is using his resources and his strength not only to the diminution of my influence, but almost to my destruction.

Diviciacus continued, confessing to Caesar, "For all that, I feel the force of brotherly love and public opinion." He explained that, "if too severe a fate befalls him at your hands, no one, seeing that I hold this place in your friendship, will opine that it has been done without *my* consent; and this will turn from me the feelings of all Gaul."

Caesar did not merely listen to the plea of Diviciacus, he "took him by the hand and consoled him." He assured Diviciacus that he felt his influence so deeply that he was willing to excuse "the injury to Rome and the vexation felt by himself, in consideration for the goodwill and entreaties of Diviciacus." Instead of publicly punishing Dumnorix, Caesar summoned him, "and in the presence of his brother . . . pointed out what he had to blame in him." Caesar warned him "to avoid all occasions of suspicion for the future," explained that he excused past treachery only out of consideration for his brother, then posted sentinels to watch over him day and night from that moment forward.

Caesar had ample military, legal, practical, and personal reason to punish Dumnorix. He had—and would—execute certain men for plotting or doing far less than Dumnorix both plotted and did. Yet his awareness of the consequences of even justified action prompted Caesar to take a different course. He did not, however, merely back down from punishment. Even less did he ignore the transgression of Dumnorix. Instead, he used purposeful forbearance of the punishment of one brother to increase the loyalty and allegiance of the other. He transformed a dangerous situation—in which the only foreseeable reward was the dubious benefit of vengeance whereas the risk was the loss of a powerful friend's influence over the hearts and minds of a fickle ally—into a magnificent opportunity for strengthening relations between Rome and its less-than-wholehearted tributary tribe.

> **Urged to action,** pause instead to anticipate all consequences, to work through the ever-present equation of reward versus risk, and to shape, modify, direct, or abandon the contemplated action accordingly. We are all too accustomed to await "results" and "deal with" them after they arrive. For Caesar, "results" were events to be anticipated rather than awaited, and they were to be managed proactively, not merely dealt with as accomplished facts. In this way, a leader seizes the future rather than accepts the often thankless task of coping with the present or the frankly hopeless task of repairing the past. Thus Caesar built an empire where none existed before.

■

Lesson 23
Refuse to Accept a Seat on the Horns of Someone Else's Dilemma

> "Ariovistus demanded that Caesar should bring no infantry with him to the parley [truce talks], as he was afraid Caesar might surround him by treachery; let each party, therefore, come with an escort of horse [cavalry]; otherwise not come at all. Caesar did not wish the parley to be broken off upon an excuse thus interposed; at the same time he could not venture to entrust his personal safety to Gallic horse."
>
> ~Julius Caesar, *The Gallic War*, Book I

Caesar was anxious to negotiate a truce or an alliance with the powerful and defiant Suebi chieftain Ariovistus. The chieftain, however, repeatedly put off such talks by setting unacceptable conditions for them. When Ariovistus finally demanded that Caesar come to the parley without a large contingent of Roman infantry as a bodyguard but only a cavalry escort—knowing that only unreliable Gallic, not fully loyal Roman, cavalry was available to Caesar—the Roman commander was faced with a dilemma. He had either to accede to Ariovistus's demand and thereby risk capture (or worse) at the hands of cavalrymen of highly questionable loyalty, or simply give up the conference he so earnestly wanted.

Invited thus to ascend the horns of a dilemma, Caesar declined to take that most uncomfortable seat. Instead, he "decided . . . that the best plan was to take the horses from Gallic troopers and mount upon them soldiers of the Tenth Legion, in which he had absolute confidence; thus, if there were need of action, he would have an escort of the truest friends he could find."

Resist all attempts to narrow your universe of action. Never assume that the either/or choices others present you with are the only possible options. Like Caesar, look for creative ways to avoid the dilemmas imposed by others. Presented with two undesirable paths, find—or build—a better third way.

Lesson 24
Probe and Prove

> "By cavalry combats . . . he sought daily to prove what the valour
> of the enemy could do and what our men could dare."
>
> ~Julius Caesar, *The Gallic War*, Book II

The Belgae were so formidable a foe, possessing (Caesar wrote) "vast numbers" and "an excellent reputation for valour," that he at first took great pains to avoid a full-scale engagement with them. This did not mean that he avoided combat, but, instead of throwing his outnumbered and quite possibly outclassed forces into a make-or-break battle, Caesar sought daily small cavalry engagements, each a probing action designed to "prove" what the enemy could actually do—not just what reputation threatened the enemy could do—and what his own men could actually "dare." The result of these probes proved the limits of the enemy's actual capacity and persuaded Caesar that "our men were not inferior" to the vaunted Belgae. He therefore prepared to commit his forces to a major battle.

"Nothing ventured, nothing gained" is such a threadbare cliché that it is easy to dismiss it without a thought. In fact, the worn old saying is still a valuable guide when you need to solve the omnipresent equation of risk versus reward. The critical step in "venturing," however, is to carefully meter what you put at risk. Actual data is always preferable to theoretical speculation, and it is therefore worth taking some risk to acquire the experience that will allow you to separate fact from assumption. Weigh the risk against the value of the data, and then venture accordingly. Caesar's approach against the Belgae was to venture modestly, day by day building factual knowledge about the capabilities of his enemy until he felt sufficient confidence to make the bold wager of all-out combat.

■

Lesson 25
The Only Authority Is Real Authority

> "The difficulties of the campaign were such as we have shown . . .
> but, nevertheless, many considerations moved Caesar to
> undertake it . . . [for] if this district were not dealt with the other
> nations might suppose they had the same liberty."
> ~Julius Caesar, *The Gallic War*, Book III

During the winter of 57–56 BCE, Caesar's fellow triumvir, Marcus Licinius Crassus, who had camped his legion among the Andes (also known as the Andecavi), one of the Iron Age Celtic tribes living on the north shore of the Bay of Biscay, fell under attack by a more powerful neighboring Celtic tribal group, the Veneti, who had enlisted as allies warriors of other local tribes. The Veneti boldly seized a number of Roman officers, who they intended to hold hostage until Crassus agreed to release Veneti and other Celtic hostages he had taken. Uncertain of how to deal with this crisis, Crassus sent word to Caesar, who was in winter quarters in Cisalpine Gaul, modern northern Italy. Caesar responded by ordering Crassus to begin building warships on the Loire River and, as he did this, to issue a warning to the Veneti that he, Caesar, was immediately journeying back to Transalpine Gaul to do battle against them.

If Caesar hoped that the mere threat of facing him as an enemy would be sufficient to intimidate the Veneti and their allies, he was doomed to disappointment. The warriors did not stand down in response to his assertion of authority, but, on the contrary, during 56 BCE, prepared to wage a full-scale war of rebellion against Roman imperialism.

Caesar fully appreciated the difficulties of undertaking a major campaign in winter and in the rugged land of the Veneti and their allies. The territory, intimately familiar to the tribes, was virtually unknown to the Romans. What they knew was that harbors, crucial to mounting and sustaining an aggressive campaign, were scarce, and supplying invading legions would therefore be difficult. The Veneti and the others had also set about fortifying their towns and building ships. They were continually adding more tribes to their alliance as well.

Despite the odds against the endeavor, Caesar counted the "detention of the Roman knights" to be "outrageous," as were "the renewal of war after surrender, the revolt after hostages given, [and] the conspiracy of so many states." Above all else, Caesar feared that if the Veneti and their allies were allowed to prevail in "this district," then "other nations might suppose they had the same liberty." Indeed, Caesar "knew well enough that almost all the Celts and Gauls were bent on revolution, and could be recklessly and rapidly aroused to war." For all of these reasons, therefore, the time had come to do more than simply assert authority backed by threat. The time had come actually to exercise authority, which meant giving authority the reality of force, no matter the difficulties involved. Caesar unleashed a high-risk, high-stakes campaign of unprecedented intensity and extent throughout Gaul.

Authority, Caesar understood, could be claimed by right and asserted in theory, but only when it was backed by credible force did it become real, and, in the end, the *only* authority is *real* authority. He therefore sought to counter the rebellion of the Veneti by boldly employing widespread force. Although the risk was very great, Caesar regarded the stakes as far greater because the action of the Veneti, already aided by numerous allies, threatened to touch off a universal revolution among the Gauls, a revolution that could undo the Gallic empire Caesar had just built.

Such titles as CEO, chairperson, manager, and director propose the theory of leadership. Only through the reality of demonstrated leadership, however, does theory acquire the substance of real authority. Caesar never rested on his titles. Caesar never rested.

■

Lesson 26
Remodel the Environment

> "Caesar set to work to cut down the forests, and, to prevent any
> flank attack on troops unarmed and unprepared, he placed all the
> timber felled on the side towards the enemy, and also piled it as a
> rampart on both flanks. With incredible rapidity, a great space
> was cleared in a few days, until the enemy's cattle and the
> rearward of their baggage were in our keeping, while [the enemy]
> themselves sought the denser forests."
>
> ~Julius Caesar, *The Gallic War*, Book III

Some enemies Caesar defeated militarily, forcing their surrender
and allowing them to live. Others he destroyed utterly. In some
cases, he deemed neither defeat of the army nor decimation of the
civilian population sufficient. When necessary, he transformed the
environment itself.

As part of what he called "the general pacification of Gaul,"
Caesar dispatched his legions to cut down vast tracts of forest,
thereby depriving the enemy of both cover and forage adjacent to
areas controlled by Rome and those tribes he deemed reliable allies.
For good measure, he used the fallen timber as a barricade between
his forces and the enemy and also as a giant fence behind which he
appropriated and enclosed what had been the enemy's cattle.

In taking Gaul, Caesar used a combination of persuasion,
genuinely beneficial mutual alliance, intimidation, violence,
terror, and genocide. Where winning over human populations
and converting political systems were insufficient to gain
absolute control, he reshaped the landscape itself.

Markets and business environments that offer the lowest
bar to entry are those you are already prepared to serve or can
readily gear up to serve. The boldest business leaders scramble
to gather this low-hanging fruit, but then they look beyond it

for ways to transform the landscape of commerce so that it will yield many new opportunities. Caesar cut down entire forests when it suited him to do so. In far more recent times, our boldest conquerors have transformed space and time through digital and social media, carving out vast new intellectual, cultural, and commercial environments.

■

Lesson 27
Don't Be a Slave to Uncertain Rumor

> "Such stories and hearsay often induce [the Gauls] to form plans upon vital questions of which they must forthwith repent; for they are the slaves of uncertain rumours, and most men reply to them in fictions made to their taste."
>
> ~Julius Caesar, *The Gallic War*, Book IV

Caesar admired much about the Gauls, especially their physical courage and military prowess, but he considered them unreliable as allies, because they were prone to "fickleness," and he judged them "capricious in forming designs." For these reasons, he believed that "no trust should be reposed in them."

This opinion was not the product of prejudice born of a sense of Roman cultural superiority. It was, rather, the result of Caesar's observation of Gallic behavior. "It is indeed a regular habit of the Gauls to compel travelers to halt, even against their will, and to ascertain what each of them may have heard or learnt upon every subject; and in the towns the common folk surround traders, compelling them to declare from what districts they come and what they have learnt there."

Caesar himself was, of course, keen on gathering intelligence, and he by no means condemned the Gauls for wanting to acquire information. His criticism was directed at their methods of obtaining intelligence and their indiscriminate processing of it. They coerced their informants, compelling them ("even against their will") and sometimes mobbing them. The result was that those they interrogated, like "most men," tended to "reply to them in fictions." Beleaguered traders and travelers told their overbearing interlocutors what they thought they wanted to hear, crafting their responses to suit what they perceived as the "taste" of their questioners. The result was tainted and unreliable information, which is worse than having no information at all.

In business, no commodity is more valuable than information. Yet no commodity is subject to so wide a range of quality—from winning to worthless to worse: downright destructive. Caesar put a very high value on information, but he was always careful to ascertain its quality before acting upon it. As he saw it, the Gauls, in contrast to his own approach, desperately sought information in bulk. Instead of careful investigation and interrogation, they engaged in rude, rough, and intimidating questioning, apparently holding their subject virtually captive until he had given them what they wanted. The result was information of poor quality—fictions fabricated by people eager to get away from a threatening and unpleasant situation.

It is a grave mistake to elicit information from sources motivated to tell you what you want to hear rather than what they actually know. No matter how much data you require, always place quality of intelligence above quantity.

Lesson 28

Make Decision and Action One and the Same

> "After this engagement was over, Caesar felt that he ought no
> longer to receive deputies nor to accept conditions from tribes
> which had sought for peace by guile and treachery, and then had
> actually begun war. He communicated to the lieutenant-generals
> and the quartermaster-general his purpose not to lose a day in
> giving battle."
>
> ~Julius Caesar, *The Gallic War*, Book IV

Caesar had avoided trusting the German ambassadors, even as he
endeavored to give the appearance of negotiating reasonably with
them (Lesson 43, "Put Trust to the Test–Cautiously"). He observed
that the enemy had no more than eight hundred cavalry while his
own men were "five thousand strong" and therefore "had nothing
to fear." Besides, the Germans had specifically asked for a truce.
"However, directly they saw our cavalry, the enemy charged, and
speedily threw our men into confusion."

If Caesar had intended to justify a war by provoking the
Germans to the first aggressive move, he had succeeded–but it is
highly unlikely that he expected his own forces, so superior in
number, to panic under surprise attack. "When our men turned to
resist, the enemy, according to their custom, dismounted, and, by
stabbing our horses and bringing down many of our troopers to
the ground, they put the rest to rout, and indeed drove them in
such panic that they did not desist from flight . . ." A number
of distinguished officers were lost in the engagement, which,
though of relatively small scale, was a humiliating defeat for Caesar.
Nevertheless–or, rather, all the more–it was a call to war.

Refusing any further parley with the Germans, "he judged it
the height of madness to wait till the enemy's forces should be
increased and their cavalry returned." He ordered his subordinates
"not to lose a day in giving battle." The next day "a large company
of Germans, which included all the principal and senior men, came

to his quarters, with a double object—to clear themselves (or so they alleged) for engaging in a battle the day before . . . and also to get what they could in respect of the truce." Caesar responded by ordering these men to be "detained." While these individuals were held where they could do no more harm, Caesar personally "led all his troops out of camp," assuming direct command of the cavalry, "which he judged to be shaken by the recent engagement."

Having decided to go to war, he went to war. There was no interval between the decision and the act. Holding the enemy delegation prisoner, he led his army into combat, taking personal command of the unit that was most badly demoralized, the cavalry. Moreover, as he wrote, he marched his army out in "triple line of columns," a *battle* formation rather than a *marching* formation. This meant that, once they caught up with the Germans, there would be no need to regroup into battle formation. They would merely have to halt and start fighting. The eight-mile march in this formation "was so speedily accomplished that Caesar reached the enemy's camp before the Germans could have any inkling of what was toward." Now it was their turn to be "struck with sudden panic by everything—by the rapidity of our approach, the absence of their own chiefs." Caesar's speed of response, the near simultaneity of the decision to fight and the fight itself, gave them "no time . . . to think, or to decide which was best—to lead their forces against the enemy, to defend the camp, or to seek safety in flight." Panic brought paralysis, and the Romans, "stung by the treachery of the day before, burst into the camp." Those among the enemy who did not immediately flee were slain; those who managed to flee were pursued. "Hearing the noise in the rear, and seeing their own folk slain, the Germans threw away their arms, abandoned their war-standards, and [fled]. . . When they reached the junction of the Meuse and the Rhine, they gave up hope of escaping" and surrendered to Caesar, who counted some 430,000 tribesmen.

The many thousands who surrendered abjectly sought Caesar's protection—from the Gauls, who (they assumed), having witnessed their defeat, would turn and attack them in mass. Thanks, then, to great speed, the telescoping of decision and action, Caesar overwhelmed his enemy, deriving all the benefits of a long and costly war in one swift battle, which did not claim the life of a single Roman.

> **The process of making** a decision may be complex, tortured, and time-consuming. It may involve multiple tests and trials, as well as meetings, consultations, and debates. Once a decision is made, however, the less time between decision and action the better. Ideally, the two—the decision rendered and the action taken—should be simultaneous. Thought may move cautiously and back and forth. Action must move immediately and in one direction only.

■

Lesson 29
Cross the Rhine

> "The Rhine marked the limit of the Roman empire; if he thought
> it unfair that the Germans should cross into Gaul against his will,
> why did he claim any imperial power across the Rhine?"
> ~Julius Caesar, *The Gallic War*, Book IV

Having defeated the German invasion of Gaul in the spring of 55 BCE (Lesson 28, "Make Decision and Action One and the Same"), Caesar "decided for many reasons that he must cross the Rhine." This choice would be as momentous as his decision to cross another river, the Rubicon, in 49 BCE, which commenced the Civil War from which Caesar emerged as the most powerful man in the Republic.

The reasons that led Caesar to cross the Rubicon (Lesson 34, "Defeat Doubt") were clear and compelling. In 55 BCE, however, it was the German objections raised to his venturing into their land that were clear and compelling. Undeniably, Caesar had chosen to trespass beyond the declared limit of the Roman Empire. In explaining his action, in Book IV of *The Gallic War*, Caesar appears to have difficulty formulating the justification for his bold but arguably unjustifiable action. There were, he writes rather vaguely, "many reasons that he must cross the Rhine," then he seems to grope in the very next sentence for the single "most cogent reason," which "was that, as he saw the Germans so easily induced to enter Gaul, he wished to make them fearful in turn for their own fortunes, by showing them that a Roman army could and durst cross the Rhine." In other words, he crossed the Rhine to demonstrate that he could cross the Rhine.

By any modern understanding of morality and international law, this "cogent reason" is whimsical, tyrannical, unjust, and unacceptable. But was it—is it—nevertheless good leadership?

Caesar saw an opportunity to demonstrate the literal boundlessness of his will to action. Crossing the Rhine was less about empire than about displaying a capacity for personal power. That display was (as Caesar writes) for the benefit of the Germans, to teach them to be "fearful . . . for their own fortunes" before they again dared to meddle in the fortunes of others. Even more, however, the expedition across the Rhine was intended to impress his own army as well as the Senate and people of Rome. Here was a leader who, again quite literally, would stop at nothing to augment the glory of Rome. What is more, here was a leader of such prodigious audacity and ability that he had no *need* to stop at anything or for anyone. Defy him, and he would stop at nothing to overcome the resistance. Follow him, and he would lead Rome to greater extent, wealth, and glory.

> **Much of leadership concerns** limits: recognizing them, heeding them, establishing them, rejecting them, and overcoming them. Some of the most difficult and most consequential leadership decisions involve choosing among these alternatives. The great leaders cross the Rhine. Undeniably, some drown midstream.

Lesson 30
Cross the Rhine—in Style

> "[Caesar] ruled it unworthy of his own and the Romans' dignity
> to cross [the Rhine] in boats. And so, although he was confronted
> with the greatest difficulty in making a bridge, by reason of the
> breadth, the rapidity, and the depth of the river, he still thought
> that he must make that effort, or else not take his army across."
>
> ~Julius Caesar, *The Gallic War*, Book IV

While some German tribes protested the injustice of Caesar's
declared intention to cross the Rhine, the Ubii, who lived along the
right bank of the Rhine, encouraged the crossing. They were, wrote
Caesar, "the only tribe beyond the Rhine which had sent deputies to
Caesar, made friendly terms, and given hostages." They wanted his
aid in resisting their enemy, the Suebi, another Rhine people, and
they told him that "even among the farthest tribes of Germany . . .
the renown and reputation of his army" was now so great "that their
own safety was secure in the prestige and the friendship of Rome."
For this reason, the Ubii "promised a large supply of boats for the
transport of his army" across the great river.

Caesar had boldly announced his intention to cross the Rhine,
and now he was being presented with the physical means of doing
just that. Caesar was bold, but not rash. He resisted the temptation to
accept the Ubii offer of boats. He wrote that he "deemed it scarcely
safe" to risk his entire army in a boat crossing, but, even more
important, he "ruled it unworthy of his own and the Romans' dignity,
to cross in boats." The only alternative was to do what Romans had
always done: bend nature itself to the will of Rome. He would
transform the landscape by building a great bridge. It was a labor of
enormous difficulty, but he resolved to "make the effort, or else not
take his army across." Caesar meticulously described what he built:

> He caused pairs of balks eighteen inches thick, sharpened a
> little way from the base and measured to suit the depth of the

river, to be coupled together at an interval of two feet. These he lowered into the river by means of rafts, and set fast, and drove home by rammers; not, like piles, straight up and down, but leaning forward at a uniform slope, so that they inclined in the direction of the stream. Opposite to these, again, were planted two balks coupled in the same fashion, at a distance of forty feet from base to base of each pair, slanted against the force and onrush of the stream. These pairs of balks had two-foot transoms let into them atop, filling the interval at which they were coupled, and were kept apart by a pair of braces on the outer side at each end. So, as they were held apart and contrariwise clamped together, the stability of the structure was so great and its character such that, the greater the force and thrust of the water, the tighter were the balks held in lock. These trestles were interconnected by timber laid over at right angles, and floored with long poles and wattlework. And further, piles were driven in aslant on the side facing down stream, thrust out below like a buttress and close joined with the whole structure, so as to take the force of the stream; and others likewise at a little distance above the bridge, so that if trunks of trees, or vessels, were launched by the natives to break down the structure, these fenders might lessen the force of such shocks, and prevent them from damaging the bridge.

The entire incredible work "was completed in ten days from that on which the collecting of timber began, and the army was taken across." Upon his crossing, as he marched into Germany, tribes rushed forward to offer "peace and friendship" (to which offers Caesar "replied in generous fashion") or they simply fled, evacuating "their territory . . . and [hiding] themselves in the remote part of the forests." Whereas he greeted with generosity those who frankly offered peace, he summarily burned all the villages from which other tribes had fled, and he set his soldiers to work cutting down their cereal crops. To those who offered friendship, he would be a friend. To those who offered defiance, he would deliver devastation. Such was the proposition of Julius Caesar.

> **Bold action is a** valuable weapon in the arsenal of leadership, but it will backfire, quite possibly with catastrophic results, if the original impulse is not followed through with stout support and brilliant engineering. The successful leadership gesture begins as an idea but is made real through determined and practical effort.

■

Lesson 31
Make the Unknown Known

> "Caesar was intent upon starting for Britain. In fact, nobody except traders journey thither without good cause; and even traders know nothing except the sea-coast and the districts opposite Gaul."
>
> ~Julius Caesar, *The Gallic War*, Book IV

By the fall of 55 BCE, Caesar had conquered Gaul and suppressed German incursions across the Rhine. Despite the imminent arrival of winter, a season in which armies did not customarily make war, "Caesar was intent upon starting for Britain."

About Britain, he knew only one thing: "that in almost all the Gallic campaigns succours had been furnished for our enemy from that quarter." For this reason alone, to cut off a source of aid to his enemies in Gaul, Caesar resolved to invade and conquer the largely mysterious island across the Channel.

He "supposed that, if the season left no time for actual campaigning, it would still be of great advantage to him merely to have entered the island, observed the character of the natives, and obtained some knowledge of the localities, the harbours, and the landing-places; for almost all these matters were unknown . . . ." Traders had some knowledge, if not of the interior, at least of "the sea-coast and the districts opposite Gaul. Therefore, . . . he summoned to his quarters traders from all parts." Yet, even after questioning them, he "could discover neither the size of the island, nor the number or strength of the tribes inhabiting it, nor their manner of warfare, nor the ordinances they observed, nor the harbours suitable for a number of large ships." Clearly, Caesar needed "to gain such knowledge before he made the venture." For this purpose, he chose one Gaius Volusenus as "a proper person to send on in advance with a ship of war. His orders were to spy out everything and to return to him at once." In the meantime, Caesar led his forces to the territory of the Morini, who lived in the region of what is today Boulogne and Calais, from which, Caesar accurately observed, "was the shortest passage across to Britain."

While Caesar waited for Gaius Volusenus to complete his mission, traders reported to the Britons his intention to make the crossing. This brought to him "deputies . . . from several states in the island with promises to give hostages and to accept the empire of Rome." Gratified that his reputation had such an effect on the Britons, Caesar politely listened to these emissaries, "made them a generous promise, encouraging them to keep their word," and then sent them back to Britain in company with Commius, the man he himself had appointed king of the Belgic tribe of the Atrebates. Because he had personally elevated Commius to supreme power among the Atrebates, Caesar was confident of the man's loyalty as well as his "courage and discretion." Caesar ordered him "to visit what states he could" in Britain and "to exhort them to seek the protection of Rome, and to announce his own speedy advent thither."

When Gaius Volusenus returned from Britain, having "observed all the country so far as was possible for an officer who did not dare to disembark and entrust himself to the rough natives,"

Caesar listened to his report and added this information, scant though it was, to intelligence he garnered from traders' stories and the words of the "deputies . . . from several states." Having done his best to transform the almost totally unknown island into an entity sufficiently glimpsed for him to risk a campaign, Caesar embarked.

Caesar's priority in any campaign was speed. He had an army to feed and to shelter. He wanted to limit their exposure as much as possible. He also regarded speed to be what modern military analysts term a "force multiplier," a factor that increases the effectiveness of a fixed number of troops, weapons, and other resources. While speed was a top priority, Caesar balanced it against the need for information. He wanted his men to run, but he was unwilling to run them into the black void of a total unknown. He took steps to make the unknown known—however incompletely. His preparations for the invasion of Britain provide an example of managing the competing imperatives a chief executive often encounters: the need to act on an opportunity before its window closes versus the need to study and understand the components, contours, risks, and rewards that opportunity represents.

■

Lesson 32
Diagnose and Cure

"Caesar noticed this; and causing the boats of the warships, and likewise the scout-vessels, to be manned with soldiers, he sent them to support any parties whom he had observed to be in distress."
~Julius Caesar, *The Gallic War*, Book IV

Modern military commanders know well that an amphibious assault—getting troops from the water onto the beach—is the most hazardous tactical operation in warfare. Caesar experienced these hazards for himself when he landed his men on Britain for the first time. Fortunately for him and for his legions, he possessed the skill of a great military manager. He observed the landing, saw a potentially fatal problem, diagnosed it, and immediately administered the cure.

Fighting was fierce, he wrote, when his troops disembarked in the vicinity of what is today Dover. Having made a difficult landing in deep water, "they could not keep rank, nor stand firm, nor follow their proper standards [banners]—for any man from any ship attached himself to whatever standard he chanced upon." Discipline was always the signal advantage of the Roman legions. In the novel situation of an amphibious assault, "considerable disorder" undermined discipline, greatly endangering the soldiers. For their part, the Britons were quick to exploit the chaos, "many surrounding few, while others hurled missiles into a whole party from the exposed flank."

"Caesar noticed this." The sight did not instill anger or panic in this commanding general, but it did set into motion his formidable powers of analysis. He quickly diagnosed the difficulty unfolding before him and, in response, loaded troops onto his small craft—boats from the warships and "scout-vessels," all craft small enough to get into the shallows or even onto the beach itself—and then sent them "to support any parties whom he had observed to be in distress."

The effect of this infusion of support was dramatic. "The moment our men stood firm on dry land, they charged with all their comrades close behind, and put the enemy to rout."

Fight the impulse to panic in the face of adversity or, what is even worse, the impulse to deny adversity. Placing blame is of no use, either. Instead, observe the crisis and identify the problem. Then *work the problem*. Manage adversity by diagnosing the difficulty and commencing the cure. Instead of blame, provide support— and provide it precisely where it is needed.

Lesson 33
Keep an Eye on Dumnorix

"Caesar had determined to keep Dumnorix in particular with him, because he knew him to be bent on revolution, bent on sovereignty, a man of great courage and of great weight among the Gauls."

~Julius Caesar, *The Gallic War*, Book V

In 58 BCE, when Caesar first entered Gaul as the governor of the province he would so vastly expand, Dumnorix, chieftain of the Aedui (who lived between what are today the Saône and Loire Rivers in France), rebelled against the Romans by conspiring with the Sequani tribe (resident in the Saône basin, the Doubs River valley, and the Jura Mountains) to allow the Celtic Helvetii tribe to migrate from what is today the Swiss plateau through their territory. Always determined to impose stability upon Gaul, Caesar had forbidden such passages and migrations, which, he believed, amounted to invasions of a Roman province. Accordingly, he dispatched forces to block the Helvetii, and he demanded that the Aedui, who had declared themselves allies of Rome, furnish wheat and other grains to the Roman soldiers. In response to this demand, Dumnorix used his influence to prevent his fellow tribal leaders from complying.

Caesar investigated thoroughly, and after securing evidence of Dumnorix's conspiracy and rebellion, he contemplated acting against him, but decided to spare Dumnorix in order to maintain the continued loyalty of his brother Diviciacus, hitherto a thoroughly reliable ally. (See Lesson 22, "Anticipate Consequences, Then Manage Them Proactively.") Nevertheless, Caesar held Dumnorix under strict surveillance.

Keeping him on a short leash proved to be a very sound decision, since, over the years, he continued to be a source of interference with Roman affairs in Gaul. At last, in the campaigns of 54 BCE, Caesar resolved to reel in Dumnorix all the way, by taking him along as a hostage on what he planned as the second Roman expedition to Britain. Caesar did not want this rebellious and ambitious figure, who he recognized as "a man of great courage and of great weight among the Gauls," out of his sight, reach, and control while he was off on his new campaign across the English Channel.

Dumnorix resisted being taken away from Gaul "by every kind of entreaty" to Caesar, "affirming now that he was unused to a voyage and feared the sea" and "that he was hindered [from leaving] on religious grounds." When Caesar stood firm, insisting that he must go, Dumnorix openly "began to stir up the [other] Gallic chieftains [who were also to accompany Caesar to Britain], drawing them aside severally and exhorting them to stay on the Continent." He "sought to frighten them by expressing apprehension that there was some reason for stripping Gaul of all her nobility: that it was Caesar's design to transport to Britain and there slaughter all whom he feared to put to death in the sight of Gaul." (There is no evidence that this was, in fact, Caesar's intention; however, Dumnorix was not being unreasonably paranoid in making these speculations.)

When these "plots were reported to Caesar by several persons," he took unspecified steps to "keep Dumnorix to his allegiance, but none the less to learn all his designs." Despite these efforts (whatever they were; for Caesar did not discuss them in his history), the chieftain made a break from Caesar's camp, taking the entire Aeduan cavalry with him. Although Caesar was on the verge of embarking for Britain, he immediately "countermanded the sailing and put off everything, and then dispatched a large detachment of [Roman] cavalry to follow him up, with orders to hale him back, and if he offered force or refused to obey, to put him to death; for he supposed that a man who had disregarded his command before his face would do nothing right-minded behind his back."

"And indeed," Caesar wrote, "when Dumnorix was summoned to return he sought to resist and defend himself by force, entreating the help of his followers and crying repeatedly that he was a free man and of a free state. The pursuers, as they were ordered, surrounded the man and dispatched him." Leaderless, "the troopers of the Aedui all returned to Caesar."

Reluctant to kill Dumnorix lest this action alienate his brother Diviciacus, who was both faithful and useful to Rome, Caesar endeavored to neutralize him by keeping him under close surveillance and, ultimately, even taking him hostage, so that he would not be free to create rebellion in Gaul during Caesar's second expedition to Britain. Only when surveillance and arrest failed did Caesar invoke the ultimate sanction. His treatment of Dumnorix is an example of the adage attributed to the ancient Chinese general and military strategist Sun Tzu and so popular with business leaders today: *Keep your friends close, and your enemies closer.*

■

Lesson 34
Defeat Doubt

> *"Iacta alea est!"*
>
> ~Julius Caesar, quoted by Suetonius, *The Twelve Caesars*

A modern traveler in northern Italy must make an effort to locate the Rubicon River near Ravenna because it is today as small and undistinguished a stream as it was when Caesar stood, lost in thought, on its northern bank in the year 49 BCE. He had been leading his army from the province he governed, Gaul, into Roman Italy proper. For a commander accustomed to taking armies up and down mountains, through man-high snowfalls, over such rivers as the wide and roiling Rhine, and across the storm-tossed hazards of the English Channel, the lazy little Rubicon, already conveniently bridged, hardly presented a physical obstacle. Nevertheless, as Plutarch noted, Caesar "became full of thought" as his forces neared the river, his "mind wavered," and he "began to go more slowly and then ordered a halt." At the stream, Plutarch writes, he stood "for a long time . . . weighed matters up silently in his own mind, irresolute between . . . two alternatives."

The Rubicon was a little river, but to Julius Caesar—and to any other Roman leader—it was also a bright red line dividing Cisalpine Gaul, part of the Gallic province Caesar had conquered and was authorized by the Roman Senate to govern, from Rome itself, which was governed by that Senate and dominated by the Senate's champion, Gnaeus Pompeius Magnus: Pompey the Great.

In company with Pompey and Marcus Licinius Crassus, Caesar had shared power in Rome's First Triumvirate, spanning 59 to 53 BCE, when Crassus was killed in battle. After that triumvir's death, Caesar and Pompey jointly governed, even as their partnership rapidly deteriorated. In 52 BCE, Pompey was elected consul without Caesar, and, from this point on, actively sought to undermine Caesar.

By agreement with Pompey, Caesar was due to resign his provincial governorships and commence his own term as consul. Pompey, however, invoked a law that obligated Caesar to disband his army during the gap between the expiration of his term as governor and the beginning of his consulship. In this space of time, Caesar understood that he would be at the mercy of Pompey and any other of his enemies. Accordingly, he appealed to the Senate either to pass legislation abolishing the interval between his two offices or allowing him to retain his army during it. The Senate responded by refusing to act, whereupon Caesar imperiously issued a demand that, if he were to be obliged to disband his legions, then the Senate must order Pompey to relinquish his army as well. Offended by both the tone and content of the demand, the Senate decreed that Caesar was to be treated as an enemy of the people of Rome if he refused to submit to whatever order the Senate handed down.

As Caesar now contemplated the little river, he well knew that Pompey had the law on his side. The Lex Cornelia Majestatis forbade any Roman general from leading an army out of the province to which he was assigned. In other words, by crossing the Rubicon, Caesar and the six thousand legionaries with him would be declaring a civil war against Pompey and the Senate. The odds of victory in such a war, Caesar also knew, were against him personally and might well prove tragic for the Roman Republic.

These two grave risks were compelling reasons to turn back from the Rubicon. There were, however, two powerful reasons to advance. First, the Senate's ultimatum would strip him of all military power. Second, Caesar was convinced that Rome was being critically misgoverned. To be sure, Caesar was driven in significant measure by a desire for glory, but he sincerely judged that avoiding risk by failing to cross the Rubicon would ultimately spell disaster for Rome. To cross it would bring all the might of the Senate down upon him and would engulf the Roman Republic in civil war, but to turn back would likely bring an end to his personal power (quite probably his life as well) and would, as he also saw it, ruin Rome.

In his biography of Caesar, Plutarch wrote that the conqueror of Gaul stood on the riverbank debating "his perplexities with his friends who were there." Plutarch wrote that he earnestly pondered "the sufferings which his crossing the river would bring upon mankind," but then "imagined the fame of the story of it." Suetonius, in his account, purported to quote Caesar's actual words to his followers: "We may still draw back; but, once across that little bridge, we shall have to fight it out." The historian then writes that a perplexed Caesar suddenly saw in the middle distance the "strikingly noble" figure of a man playing upon a shepherd's pipe. The melody was so enchanting that it drew soldiers as well as the legions' trumpeters closer to hear. Of a sudden, the man laid aside his pipe, seized a trumpet from the hands of one of Caesar's military musicians, and used it to blow the traditional call to advance, crossing the Rubicon as he did so. This (Suetonius wrote) prompted Caesar to declare: "Let us accept this as a sign from the Gods, and follow where they beckon, in vengeance on our double-dealing enemies. *Iacta alea est!*"

"The die is cast!" Caesar called out (we are told) as he boldly crossed the Rubicon.

From the perspective of more than two thousand years of historical hindsight, the audacious decision seems also to have been manifestly the correct decision. It not only saved Caesar's authority—and almost certainly his life—but greatly augmented his power, elevating him, for a time, to the status of the most consequential figure in the Roman world. What is more, mired as it was in corruption under Pompey and the Senate, Rome was in precipitous decline, and Caesar now gave the state new life. Caesar's critics have claimed that he began the destruction of the Roman Republic—which would soon be replaced by a hereditary monarchy—but his reinvigoration of the state can also be seen as having given Rome and, with it, Greco-Roman culture and civilization, another four centuries of hegemony in the West and six more in the East. The effect on global civilization is, of course, still felt today.

By any measure, the decision to cross the Rubicon was of epochal consequence. We are left to speculate, however, as to just what it was in Caesar that guided and enabled him to bring himself to the decision.

The accounts of Caesar's first two biographers, Plutarch (46–120 CE) and Suetonius (69–after 122 CE), agree on at least one crucial aspect of the decision-making process. It was not impulsive. Both ancient historians imply that Caesar devoted careful thought to the consequences of civil war and that he consulted about the decision with his trusted comrades in arms.

Neither early biographer attempts to reconstruct Caesar's actual thought process, but we may try. For it is clear that while Caesar understood that crossing the Rubicon would have definite consequences, it is also apparent that he understood the equally definite consequences of failing to cross. Turning back from the river would keep the peace, but it would be a peace dictated by

Pompey and the Senate. That means that it would be a surrender, one by which Caesar would yield his power, glory, and—quite probably—his life, but, even more, a surrender that would forsake the power, glory, and even the life of Rome itself.

Win or lose, war always costs blood. That is a given of warfare. In the best case, you gain a bloody victory. In the worst, a bloody defeat. But surrender? Its only possible outcome is loss.

Cast the die—"roll the dice," as we would say today—and you may lose or you may win. Cling to the dice, however, and winning is not an option. The die uncast—the dice held tightly in the fist—provides the illusion of safety, but, in the end, had Caesar failed to act, the illusion would soon have been shattered. The decision to inaction would have been revealed as unreasonable because it was self-destructive. The *reasonable* decision—a civil war fought against the apparent odds—was hardly the safe decision, but the risks, grave as they were, had to be accepted. It was the only reasonable course, the only path toward possible salvation and possible gain.

■

Lesson 35
Plan on the Fly

> "Fearing lest his right wing should be surrounded by the multitude of [Pompey's larger] cavalry, [Caesar] hastily withdrew individual cohorts from the third line and out of these constructed a fourth line, stationing it opposite [his] cavalry, explaining what his object was and reminding them that the day's victory depended on the valour of these cohorts."
>
> ~Julius Caesar, *Civil Wars*, Book III

As explained in Lesson 36 ("Success–Make Sure Your Organization Really Wants It"), Caesar, in deploying his forces at the decisive Battle of Pharsalus (August 9, 48 BCE), essentially mirrored the formation of his enemy, Pompey. There was one exception to this mirror image– which was not only a stroke of genius, but not part of Caesar's original plan. When he actually beheld the superior size of Pompey's cavalry, Caesar feared that his right would be surrounded and overwhelmed by it. On the fly, in immediate response to what he observed, Caesar radically altered his plan, pulling infantrymen out of his own already thin third line and (as he himself said) "hastily" improvised a fourth line, which he positioned not as part of the infantry, but just opposite his cavalry, to support a unit he knew was in danger.

Caesar fully appreciated that his outnumbered horsemen were vulnerable. More importantly, he knew that Pompey the Great realized this as well. He reasoned that his rival would inevitably attack what appeared to be a target both ripe and easy. He therefore resolved to use his cavalry, which he commanded personally, as bait to draw the overconfident cavalry of Pompey into a surprise counterattack by the concealed fourth line of infantry.

In theory, it was a brilliant improvisation. Caesar well knew, however, that battles are not won theoretically but in the reality of execution. Leaving nothing to chance, therefore, he took valuable time to explain to the men he had moved into the fourth line precisely "what his object was," and, having given the explanation, laid out the stakes he was entrusting to them, "reminding them that the day's victory depended on [their] valour."

It takes skill to create a business plan. It takes both creativity and courage to alter that plan effectively when reality demands an adaptive alteration. Such a real-time improvisation must still be treated as a plan, albeit a plan drawn up on the fly, which means that, even in haste, it must be thought through and thoroughly explained.

Lesson 36
Success—Make Sure Your Organization Really Wants It

"They wanted it; even after all my great deeds I, Caius Caesar, would have been condemned, if I had not sought support from my army."

~Julius Caesar, as he surveyed the enemy dead after the
Battle of Pharsalus, August 9, 48 BCE

After barely surviving the Battle of Dyrrachium (July 10, 48 BCE), Caesar found himself continually shadowed by his rival Pompey the Great, who avoided pitched battle in a campaign of attrition aimed at starving Caesar and his forces into defeat. At Thessaly, however, senators who formed part of Pompey's faction protested their champion's inglorious approach to war. They demanded that he offer a gallant showdown battle. Pompey protested, but ultimately caved into the pressure, and on August 9, 48 BCE (as figured by the calendar in force at the time; most historians believe the battle actually took place in June), he accepted battle near Pharsalus, in southern Thessaly, Greece.

Caesar was leading troops in whom he had utmost confidence. Three of his legions, recruited specifically for the Civil War and therefore raw, were anchored by four veteran legions of the Gallic Wars, including his favorite X Equestris (Tenth Legion). Caesar had every reason to believe that his army was highly motivated and wanted victory above all else and at all cost. On the other hand, all of his legions were short-handed, having suffered losses at Dyrrachium and also because Caesar had decided to advance into combat with a smaller body of handpicked men instead of larger, but more ponderous and less reliable forces. He consciously and purposefully traded sheer numbers to gain valor and commitment.

Still, all the quantifiable tactical advantages rested with Pompey the Great. He had more men, he occupied higher ground, and he enjoyed an unbroken line of supply. Caesar understood this, but he also knew his opponent well. He correctly assumed that, enjoying obvious advantages, Pompey would continue even now, in open battle, to carry out his conservative and conventional approach to war. In his younger years, Pompey had been a great general; much older now, he had traded boldness for competence, and this quality, admirable though it was, made him eminently predictable. Caesar observed as Pompey deployed his army in the prescribed manner, forming his troops into three lines, each ten men deep. Caesar correctly assumed that, following convention, Pompey would position his best legions on the flanks, with raw recruits making up the center. By Caesar's calculation, Pompey had 45,000 men (modern historians believe he may have actually commanded between 40,000 and 60,000), and he was well aware that his own strength was a mere 22,000. He therefore sought to ratchet up the determination of his forces by pointing out to his troops that they were out of supplies and had no clear lines of retreat. Defeat, he argued, would mean slaughter. His logic was as brutal as it was inescapable: If you want to live, you must want victory.

Like Pompey, Caesar formed his men in three lines, mirroring the configuration of the enemy. He could afford a depth of just six men, however, since he needed to extend his lines as far out as Pompey's, lest the enemy make a devastating flanking attack. Both armies had the Enipeas River to their south (which was Pompey's right flank, Caesar's left), so both concentrated their cavalry units on their north flanks, to give the horsemen freedom of movement. Caesar, however, took the boldly unconventional step of thinning out his already comparatively sparse infantry ranks to create a small fourth line of foot soldiers as a backup for his cavalry. Pompey had no such infantry support for his cavalry—it wasn't in the books. Caesar, furthermore, assumed direct command of the cavalry, which gave him maximum mobility on the battlefield.

Caesar relates that there was great distance between the opposing armies. Pompey chose to avoid charging, compelling Caesar's forces to advance toward him—thereby (Pompey believed) exhausting themselves. Indeed, Caesar did order a charge, and his army obeyed, but, observing that Pompey's forces did not advance to meet them, Caesar's infantry commanders, acting on their own initiative, ordered a halt and a rest. Far from later criticizing his subordinates for acting without orders, Caesar praised them for having exercised both sound judgment and great discipline. To him, it was clear that his troops *wanted* victory.

When at last the battle commenced in earnest, Pompey's cavalry commander, Titus Labienus (at one time a Caesar loyalist), ordered an attack that pushed back Caesar's much smaller cavalry. Caesar's fourth line of infantry, positioned behind his cavalry, was unknown to Labienus. As Caesar led his cavalry in retreat, he suddenly unleashed the supporting infantry. They employed against Labienus an entirely novel tactic, in which Caesar had carefully trained them. Instead of hurling their javelins—the conventional mode of using this weapon—they wielded them as spears, directing them against the unprotected faces of the cavalry troopers. The combination of the surprise infantry attack and the stunningly unconventional method of the attack threw Pompey's cavalry into a chaos of panic. Not only did they depart the field, they left Pompey's left flank—the infantry—completely exposed. Now Caesar led his cavalry, together with its supporting infantry, against Pompey's left, smashing through and thereby getting behind his lines. While the cavalry and its infantry support wheeled about to attack Pompey from the rear, Caesar not only continued his frontal attack with his first two main lines of infantry, but committed his third line, which was still fresh, to combat. The effect was overwhelming, and Pompey's army, though at least twice the size of Caesar's, retreated in complete disorder.

At this point, the Battle of Pharsalus was as good as over. Pompey had withdrawn into his camp as soon as he saw the rout of his cavalry. This left the bulk of his army effectively leaderless. Commanding the garrison to defend the camp, he fled. Although the garrison fought on valiantly, Caesar's men overran the camp and annihilated its defenders. By the time the battle was ended and

Caesar surveyed the carnage, anywhere between 6,000 and 15,000 Pompeian troops lay dead (another 24,000 would be captured), whereas Caesar counted just 200 soldiers and 30 centurions among his fallen. Pompey made good his escape to Egypt, but he found no asylum there. In September, he would be assassinated on the order of Pharaoh Ptolemy XIII, who sought to curry favor with Caesar.

The Battle of Pharsalus made Caesar's triumph in the Civil War virtually a foregone conclusion, although combat, led by Pompey's two sons and other Pompeians, continued fitfully for several more years.

One of the most consequential battles in all of history, Pharsalus was a triumph of quality over quantity. Not only did Caesar defeat Pompey by tactical superiority—personally commanding the cavalry, unconventionally supporting the cavalry with infantry, training the infantry to fight in a novel and devastating manner—but also through superiority of motivation. He handpicked men who had demonstrated a record of *wanting* victory, and he put them in a position to *want* that victory even more desperately.

Everyone knows that creativity and passion are important, but who could possibly know just how much they count toward achieving success? Caesar knew—or did he only guess?—that these would multiply the effectiveness of an army by at least a factor of two.

■

Negotiation and Persuasion

Lesson 37
Give Everyone a Stake

> "Upon conclusion of the Helvetian campaign deputies from well-nigh the whole of Gaul, the chief men of the various states, assembled in Caesar's camp to congratulate him. They perceived, they said, that, although Caesar had by the campaign required satisfaction of the Helvetii for past outrages suffered by the Roman people at their hands, the result had been as beneficial to the land of Gaul as to the Roman people."
>
> ~Julius Caesar, *The Gallic War*, Book I

History records Julius Caesar as the conqueror of Gaul, and while Caesar himself wanted his fellow Romans to see him as just that, he was careful to avoid giving this impression to the people of Gaul itself. Instead, he worked tirelessly to create and cement alliances with various tribes, securing from them everything from outright military aid to simple non-interference as he fought the groups and individuals who refused to yield to Rome. He wrote frequently of winning whenever possible by "policy" instead of "the sword," and he made it his policy to give others a stake in *his* victory.

In the case of his war against the Helvetii, Caesar was able to persuade numerous Gallic tribes that the Germanic people constituted a common enemy to Gaul and Rome alike. Caesar thus presented himself not as a conqueror but as a liberator by demonstrating to the Gauls that the Helvetii meant to make "war upon the whole of Gaul," thereby "obtaining an empire." Caesar was not so frank as to explain that his intention was likewise imperial. But he did not have to. It was sufficient for him to define Rome's enemy, the Helvetii, as imperialist invaders, while he painted himself and his legions as something else: friends.

> **Shared benefit is always** a better motivator than implied or delivered threat. Common cause is a source of creative energy, whereas division consumes resources. The most enduring conquests are the products of building up rather than tearing down. Approach others not with a hand out or, even less, a fist raised, but with hands full of a good offer.

■

Lesson 38
Recognize a Need, Offer Value

"Caesar comforted the Gauls with his words, promising that he would concern himself with this matter."

~Julius Caesar, *The Gallic War*, Book I

Called by Caesar *rex Germanorum*, "king of the Germans," Ariovistus was a leader of the Suebi tribe and its allies and, long before Caesar's arrival, had entered Gaul in some measure as a conqueror and yet also in some measure as an ally of the Gauls, marrying into a Gallic tribe (without, however, renouncing his Suebian wife). Before Caesar became governor of Gaul, the Roman Senate, seeking an alliance, acknowledged Ariovistus a king. He had, after all, leagued with the Arverni and Sequani, both Gallic tribes, to suppress the Celtic Aedui in the upper Loire River basin of France. As a result of what Caesar called the Battle of Magetobriga—fought before his arrival in Gaul—Ariovistus defeated the Aedui, who thereby became subject to the Sequani. His Sequani allies remitted to Ariovistus fully a third of the Aeduan territory, on which he settled some 120,000 Germans. This resettlement accomplished, he turned against his former allies, the Sequani, by demanding that they yield to him the entire Doubs valley in what is today eastern France and western Switzerland. This was the situation as it stood when Caesar arrived in Gaul as the Roman governor of the province.

In 58 BCE, after defeating the Helvetii, Caesar was approached by Diviciacus the Aeduan, who told him of how Ariovistus exercised "a proud and cruel tyranny, demanding as hostages the children of the greatest nobles, and perpetrating upon them all the direst forms of torture, if anything be not performed at his nod or his pleasure. He is a passionate, a reckless barbarian," Diviciacus declared. "We can endure his tyrannies no longer."

Seeing an opportunity to cement an alliance with one set of peoples in order to evict another—both circumstances that furthered his goal of conquest in Gaul—Caesar recognized a need and offered a value in answer to that need. Won over by his proposition, Diviciacus aligned the Aeduans and other Gallic tribes with Rome; however, Caesar noted "that of all the company the Sequani alone did not act like the rest, but with head downcast stared sullenly upon the ground."

The "lot of the Sequani," Diviciacus explained to Caesar, "is more pitiable, more grievous than that of the rest." Whereas the other tribes could negotiate with Caesar in the knowledge that they had a means of escaping the wrath of Ariovistus if need be, the Sequani were trapped because they had already "admitted Ariovistus within their borders" and their towns "are all in his power." If he discovered they had complained to Caesar, they "must needs endure any and every torture."

In the challenge presented by this dilemma Caesar saw only greater opportunity. Telling the Sequani that "he would concern himself with this matter," he proposed to use "his good offices and his authority" to "induce Ariovistus to put a stop to his outrages." Caesar next sent an embassy to summon Ariovistus to a conference. When Ariovistus refused to come, Caesar replied with a demand that he bring no more of his people across the Rhine into Gaul and that he restore all hostages to the Aedui. Fail to do these things, Caesar warned, and Ariovistus would lose the friendship of Rome.

This time, Ariovistus not only refused to comply, but defiantly dared Caesar to attack him. It was precisely what Julius Caesar wanted: grounds to further his war of conquest in Gaul—and to do so not merely in the name of Rome, but in what purported to be the defense of Rome's allies, the Aedui and Sequani, who had, after all, requested his aid.

> **The need of others** is an opportunity for you. Caesar was a master at exploiting division among peoples, factions, and tribes, using it to pit one group against another in order to propel his own interests forward. Caesar never *asked* for support. Instead, he *persuaded* others of their urgent need to offer him support and in this way was carried to the conquest of Gaul.

■

Lesson 39
Argue Against Panic

"So great was the panic, and so suddenly did it seize upon all the army, that it affected in serious fashion the intelligence and the courage of all ranks."

~Julius Caesar, *The Gallic War*, Book I

Having identified the fortress town of Vesontio in eastern France as the key to holding the territory of the Sequani against conquest by Ariovistus, the renegade chieftain of the Germanic Suebi tribe, Caesar force-marched his army day and night to seize and hold this objective. All was well until Caesar halted just outside of Vesontio to resupply his army. Suddenly, "a panic arose from inquiries made by our troops and remarks uttered by Gauls and traders, who affirmed that the Germans were men of a mighty frame and an incredible valour and skill at arms; for they themselves (so they said) at meetings with the Germans had often been unable even to endure their look and the keenness of their eyes."

A demonic mythology was born in an instant, and the panic grew until it swept over the whole army, so "that it affected in serious fashion the intelligence and the courage of all ranks." As the irrational fear spread like a contagion ("even men who had long experience in the field, soldiers, centurions, and cavalry commanders, were gradually affected"), Caesar took action, convening a council of war to which he summoned the centurions, the officers equivalent to the company commanders of a modern army, each of whom led a century, which, despite the name, typically consisted of eighty, not a hundred, men.

As was right and proper, Caesar began by reprimanding the centurions for daring to question his command authority; however, he did not leave the issue there. After thus laying down the law by reaffirming the unalterably absolute nature of the military chain of command, thereby countering panic with authority–chaos with order–Caesar continued his address to the troops by applying reason as an antidote to the irrational speculation and rumor that were the sources of that runaway emotion known as panic. He began by asserting the utter irrationality of assuming that Ariovistus, a sworn friend of Rome, would casually abandon his duty to Rome, especially after he, Caesar, had offered him eminently fair and generous terms of an alliance. Having declared his disbelief that Ariovistus would recklessly "reject the goodwill of myself or the Roman people," Caesar took another rhetorical step. Even if–against all reason–Ariovistus did decide to rebel, Caesar discounted the gravity of the resulting consequences. What "have you to fear?" he asked his men. "Why do you despair of your own courage or of my competence?" After all, he pointed out, "We have made trial of this foe in the time of our fathers" and defeated them. "We have made further trial of late in Italy in the slave revolt," and the slaves (Caesar reminded his centurions) had "practice and training . . . learnt from us." They had the skill of Roman soldiers–a skill these barbarians lack.

Caesar reserved his most logically potent argument for last: "Finally," he declared, "these are the selfsame men with whom the Helvetii have had frequent encounters, and they have often subdued them, not only in Helvetian territory but also in Germany; yet the Helvetii have not proved a match for *our* army."

To defeat panic, Caesar offered strong syllogistic logic. If you have defeated the army that defeated the enemy you now face, you can certainly defeat that lesser force. The conclusion, virtually inescapable, was not one Caesar imposed on his men. It was a conclusion he made it possible for them to reach. Caesar understood what all remarkably persuasive people understand. The most compelling ideas are those we think of as our own.

> **Rumor, demoralization, unthinking fear.** These are highly destructive to any enterprise, especially one engaged in a competitive marketplace or environment. Do not ignore panic. While it may help to assert your official authority in the face of irrational emotion, do not rely on the tenuous strength of your job description. The most effective counter to the abandonment of reason is reason applied compellingly to verifiable fact. *Argue* your organization out of panic.
>
> Here is the formula: Add to reason a large dose of likelihood and the record of past performance. Apply liberally.
>
> It is not unusual for individuals and organizations to lose their nerve in the face of the unknown, which is, after all, a vacuum that the vulnerable imagination rushes to fill. Displace fearful imagining with reasonable assumption. Displace rumor and imagination with the verifiable facts of actual precedent. Then step back and allow the members of your organization to draw their own—inevitable—conclusions.

Lesson 40
Make Yourself Indispensable

> "He would do, he said, what he had done in the case of the Nervii,
> and command the neighbors to do no outrage to the surrendered
> subjects of Rome."
>
> ~Julius Caesar, *The Gallic War*, Book II

When, overawed by Caesar's demonstration of his magnificent siege tower, the Belgic warriors of Aduatuci tribe followed those of the Nervii in abject surrender to Rome, they sought only a single condition: "if haply of his mercy and kindness . . . Caesar decided to save the Aduatuci alive," they beseeched him not to "despoil them of their arms. Almost all their neighbours," they explained, "were at enmity with them . . . and . . . if they delivered up their arms, they could not defend themselves. If they were to be brought into such case, it were better for them to suffer any fortune at the hand of Rome than to be tortured and slain by men among whom they were accustomed to hold mastery."

It was an understandable and reasonable request, with which Caesar clearly sympathized. He responded to it, however, by telling the Aduatuci emissaries that although he would "save their state alive" because "they surrendered before the battering-ram touched the wall," he could grant "no terms of surrender save upon delivery of arms."

On the face of it, this was a fatal condition, which the Aduatuci probably could not accept. Caesar, however, understood what happens when you leave a defeated people with nothing to lose. They fight like men with nothing to lose. After delivering what seemed to be an unacceptable ultimatum, he continued, pledging that he "would do . . . what he had done in the case of the Nervii, and command the neighbours to do no outrage to the surrendered subjects of Rome." The Aduatuci negotiators took these terms back "to their tribesmen," who agreed to them. Caesar and his soldiers watched as a "great quantity of arms was cast from the wall into the trench which was before the town, so that the heaps of weapons were well-nigh level with the top of the wall."

> **The terms Caesar dictated** for peace were not a simple exchange of value—give us your territory, and we will spare your lives—but something far more durable and enduring: a relationship of dependence. Caesar created conditions that made the Aduatuci dependent on Rome. He made Rome neither abjectly feared nor merely tolerated among the Aduatuci, but absolutely indispensable to them. The great object of any negotiation is to make yourself indispensable to the other side. Settle for nothing short of this relationship.

■

Lesson 41
Instead of an Ultimatum, Offer an Alternative

"He could have no friendship with them, if they remained in Gaul. . . . However, they had permission, if they pleased, to settle in the territories of the Ubii."

~Julius Caesar, *The Gallic War*, Book IV

When Caesar learned that various Gallic tribes had sent envoys across the Rhine into the territory of the Germans, "inviting them to leave the Rhine, and promising to furnish all things demanded of them" so that they might settle in Gaul, he decided that the only way to preempt what threatened to become an outright invasion that would undercut Roman control of Gaul was to "make war on the Germans." Accordingly, Caesar resolved to make an expedition across the Rhine, into the country of the Germans.

As Caesar approached the Rhine, he was met by a German delegation, which condemned the Roman advance as precisely what it was: a provocation. "The Germans," they said, "did not take the first step in making war on the Roman people"; however, they warned, they would not "refuse the conflict of arms" if provoked, "for it was the ancestral custom of the Germans to resist anyone who made war upon them." They continued: "if the Romans would have their [German] goodwill," let them "either grant them lands, or suffer them to hold the lands their arms had acquired."

Caesar listened to the delegation. He must have realized that the German ambassadors were actually quite correct in their assertion that he, not they, was provoking war; nevertheless, he replied with what began as a harsh ultimatum: "He could have no friendship with them, if they remained in Gaul." In other words, either leave Gaul and enjoy peace, or remain in Gaul and suffer war. No sooner did he issue the ultimatum, however, than he softened the edges of its absoluteness by explaining the basis of his reasoning: "there was no land in Gaul which could be granted without injustice" to the Gauls. This said, he took yet another step back from demand and threat by replacing the ultimatum with a voluntary alternative. The Germans, he said, "had permission, if they pleased, to settle in the territories of the Ubii, whose deputies were in his camp, complaining of the outrages of the Suebi and seeking his assistance." This being the case, Caesar implied, he was in a position to "give orders to the Ubii" that they admit the Germans into their territory. The envoys did not respond to this alternative immediately, but they promised to report the offer to their people.

> **Sustainable business succeeds through** the exchange of value for value. To be sure, it is possible to force rivals into defeat or to take advantage of market conditions to compel customers to pay very high prices for what they want. But such zero-sum game approaches to business destroy rather than build the relationships necessary to sustain success over the long term. You cannot partner with a dead rival, nor can you expect repeat business from a customer who feels coerced. Caesar made use

of harsh ultimatums when he felt he had no other choice. Far preferable to him, however, was to offer an alternative instead of an ultimatum. Without question, his goal was to make Rome preeminent among nations and people. Yet he believed this could be achieved more efficiently and completely by offering other nations and other people sufficient value to induce them voluntarily to yield to Rome rather than to defy Rome and thereby invite a costly war to annihilate them.

Offering value to others does not require abandoning your goal of achieving supremacy in your market or field. On the contrary, it facilitates your journey toward this goal. When your wants and needs conflict with those of another, emulate Caesar by identifying and offering an alternative to the zero-sum outcome of an ultimatum.

■

Lesson 42
Don't Trust; Manage

> "Caesar replied that he could not even grant that request."
> ~Julius Caesar, *The Gallic War*, Book IV

To the German invaders of Gaul, Caesar offered settlement among the Ubii tribe, which was beholden to him (Lesson 41, "Instead of an Ultimatum, Offer an Alternative"). The response of the German delegation that came to him was promising. They announced that they would report his offer to their people "and, after deliberation upon the matter, return to Caesar in three days." During that time, "they asked him not to move his camp nearer" the Rhine. Flattered and encouraged by the apparently positive response to his offer, a lesser man might have given the ambassadors their three days.

Not Julius Caesar.

"Caesar replied that he could not even grant that request." He did not reveal to the ambassadors that he "knew, in fact, that [the Germans] had sent a large detachment of cavalry some days before to the country of the Ambivariti across the Meuse, to get booty and corn [cereal crops]" and that "he supposed that [the Germans] were waiting for [the return of] this cavalry, and for that reason sought to interpose delay." Caesar resisted what must have been a powerful temptation to call out the ambassadors in their obvious lie. Instead, he simply refused to grant the delay and continued his advance on the German home territory.

> **Trust is indispensable in** an active partnership, but trust is too much to demand when one rival (or potential rival) makes a proposal to another. Never—not in the name of "trust," "goodwill," or "good faith"—relinquish or even suspend your tactical or strategic advantage. In the absence of a working relationship of mutual profit, make no concession or sacrifice of any kind. To do so would be to accord a potential enemy control over your resources and options. This would mean surrendering before battle even commenced.

■

Lesson 43
Put Trust to the Test—Cautiously

> "Caesar supposed that all these pleas had the same object as before, to secure by a three days' interval the return of their absent cavalry; however, he said that on that day he would advance no further than four miles, in order to get water."
>
> ~Julius Caesar, *The Gallic War*, Book IV

In dealing with the Germanic tribes who threatened to invade Gaul, Caesar withheld his trust from them, declining their request for a three-day truce to answer a proposal and instead continuing his advance on the German homeland (Lesson 42, "Don't Trust; Manage"). The German ambassadors caught up with Caesar as he continued his advance, once again beseeching him to march no farther toward the Rhine. When Caesar again refused their request, "they asked him to send forward to the cavalry in advance of his column and to prevent them from engaging, and to grant themselves an opportunity of sending deputies into the land of the Ubii," among whom Caesar had said they could settle. "They put forward the hope that, if the chiefs and the senate of the Ubii pledged their faith on oath, they (the Germans) would accept the terms which Caesar offered; and they asked him to give them an interval of three days to settle these affairs."

Caesar was not buying it. He assumed that the ambassadors were seeking three more days to await the arrival of their cavalry so that they could attack the Romans in strength. Nevertheless, he decided this time to test the degree to which he *might* trust the Germans. Although he refused to stand still for three days, he told the ambassadors that he would advance on this day no more than four miles—and only to get water. He further instructed the ambassadors to meet him four miles hence on the "next day with as large a number as they could, in order that he might take cognizance of their demands."

Intending to continue his advance against the Germans, Caesar nevertheless responded to the ambassadors in a way that suggested willingness to compromise. In fact, he simply continued his march toward the Rhine. Indeed, realistically, four miles was a respectable march for an army in the space of a day. He had thus positioned himself to give the appearance of responding positively to the Germans without actually giving up anything substantive. To his own front-line commanders, he sent instructions to continue going forward, but "not to provoke the enemy to an engagement, and, if provoked themselves, to hold their ground until he himself with the [main part of] the army had come up nearer." Thus, while facilitating his own advance, Caesar prepared to hold the Germans close to their own border.

Negotiation implies movement. If you engage in talks but are determined to avoid a deal—an exchange of value for value—you may be bullying or attempting to bully, but you are not negotiating. Negotiation, however, should not require your movement to be retrograde—a retreat. Any decision you make should carry with it the expectation of a benefit, a reward. If you are negotiating with someone in whom you have little trust, ensure that the move you offer to make entails minimal negative impact on you and leaves you free to act to your benefit; however, devise a move that gives the appearance of benefiting the other person. Make *him* move to *your* advantage, even as you continue to gauge his worthiness of your trust.

■

Lesson 44
Make Yourself Look More Than Fair

> "Caesar complained that, though of their own motion they had sent deputies on to the Continent to seek peace from him, they had now begun war on him without cause; but he agreed to pardon their ignorance."
>
> ~Julius Caesar, *The Gallic War*, Book IV

After the short, sharp battle that erupted upon Caesar's landing on Britain, the tribal warriors were sufficiently intimidated to send "deputies to Caesar to treat for peace, promising that they would give hostages and do what he commanded." These emissaries were accompanied by Commius the Artebatian (see Lesson 31, "Make the Unknown Known"), the Gallic chieftain Caesar had sent as his own ambassador in advance of his landing. Instead of being treated as an emissary, however, the Britons had seized him and had clapped him in chains. Now, to Caesar's face, the deputies "cast the blame of the misdeed"—meaning the battle as well as the mistreatment of Commius—"upon the multitude, and sought pardon in consideration of their ignorance."

It was, of course, a very lame excuse, which Caesar could have chosen to reject. But he did no such thing.

Caesar made an elaborate show to the emissaries of complaining that, having sailed across the English Channel to make peace overtures to him before he even left Gaul for Britain, the Britons subsequently began "a war on him without cause" as soon as he landed. This complaint could well have served as a predicate for punitive action. Instead, Caesar chose to use it as the platform from which he "agreed to pardon [the] ignorance" of the Britons and attempt to engage them in peace.

Julius Caesar came to Britain as an invader. This fact notwithstanding, he presented himself as a man of peace who had suffered a grave offense at the hands of British warriors who did anything but welcome him and his legions to the island. The purpose of his presentation was not to justify invasion in the eyes of the world. The world of Caesar was one in which invasion figured as an acceptable instrument of empire, and Caesar would have felt no necessity to justify it. Instead, Caesar portrayed himself as a well-meaning leader wronged, and he did this to elevate the position from which he negotiated terms with the Britons. He sought to make whatever he offered appear unusually generous: quite literally *more* than fair.

Caesar had—and would yet—show himself capable of harshly punitive action. More often, however, he preferred to offer value and benefit to those peoples he wanted to incorporate within the Roman sphere, and he was eager to magnify the appearance of value and benefit however he could. It was and remains a timeless principle and tactic of deal making.

Lesson 45
Ride Your Reputation

> "The day was theirs had there been anyone among them to take it."
>
> ~Julius Caesar, *Civil Wars*, Book III

When he began the civil war by which he ultimately wrested control of Rome from Pompey the Great, Caesar led numerically inferior forces that were inadequately supplied. He himself, however, was armed with a reputation for military genius and an uncanny ability to lure his enemies into hopeless traps. Gnaeus Pompeius Magnus—Pompey the Great—along with much of the Senate that supported him against Caesar's popular insurrection, fled to Greece in 49 BCE before the approach of his former co-triumvir's army. Pompey's plan was to build up vastly superior forces in Greece, so as to ensure his ability not merely to defeat Caesar but to annihilate him. For his part, Caesar was powerless to pursue Pompey because he had no fleet. Instead of immediately proceeding to build ships, however, Caesar decided to consolidate his hold over the western Mediterranean, especially Spain.

In the meantime, Pompey assigned his naval commander, Marcus Calpurnius Bibulus, to create a great naval blockade that would prevent Caesar from crossing to Greece once his fleet was built and, at the same time, to block aid and reinforcements from reaching Caesar in Italy. Pompey counted on having plenty of time to build up his land forces since it would take Caesar a long while to construct his fleet. Caesar easily calculated that this would be Pompey's assumption, and he therefore decided to cross the Adriatic in the winter—a season when no one dared such a crossing—and with only half of his fleet built. The surprise caught Bibulus unawares, and the first contingent of Caesar's ships easily ran the blockade; however, Bibulus quickly recovered and scrambled to close the holes in his blockade. This successfully prevented the rest of Caesar's fleet, small and incomplete as it was, from making the Adriatic crossing.

The efforts of Bibulus on behalf of Pompey the Great were truly heroic, and they apparently cost him his life. The man literally worked himself to death by his labors to block Caesar. The result, however, was that Caesar was cut off on Epirus, a region that straddles what are today Albania and Greece. Isolated as he was, Caesar commanded no more than half of his army and was totally without a source of supply by sea. He decided, accordingly, to hunker down, fortify his position as best he could, and send out foraging parties to keep him and his men alive. In contrast to his rival's dire straits, Pompey had managed to amass a huge army–though the majority of the soldiers were untested recruits, whereas Caesar's much smaller forces consisted of battle-hardened veterans.

Pompey had earned his sobriquet, "the Great," through a long series of stunning victories. But those were fought when he was young. Now, at fifty-seven, he was, by Roman standards, an old man, and, with age, came caution. He was unwilling to provoke a decisive pitched battle with the vastly outnumbered Caesar and instead decided to maneuver so as to keep his rival bottled up in Epirus until the want of sustenance and supplies would starve him into submission. For his part, Caesar repeatedly sought peace talks with his former ally and fellow triumvir, but to no avail. It was only thanks to the fortitude and loyalty of his legions that Julius Caesar held out until his loyal friend Marc Antony was able to fight through Pompey's naval blockade and bring reinforcements.

As soon as he was reinforced, Caesar moved aggressively against Pompey, whose army was firmly ensconced in a formidable position south of Dyrrachium (modern Durrës, Albania). With the sea behind him and his forces surrounded by hills, Pompey the Great felt entirely secure against any direct assault. Caesar accepted the impossibility of taking Pompey's position by storm and resolved instead to lay siege to his army by constructing a great wall around it. His intention was to cut off all water for Pompey's men and all pasturage for his horses. In response, Pompey built a wall of his own parallel to Caesar's. It was a standoff, anticipating in the long fullness of history the Western Front of World War I, in which great armies fought in bloody deadlock across the interval that separated their elaborate trenches. The salient question in the siege of 48 BCE was the same as that in the war of 1914–18: Which side would be the first to break?

Pompey had a stroke of luck when he became the beneficiary of intelligence supplied by a traitor from Caesar's ranks. The man informed him of a vulnerability in Caesar's wall. Quick to exploit this, Pompey led a spectacular attack that routed Caesar's army. Now events had reached one of those moments on which history turns. All that was left was for Pompey to capitalize on his breakthrough by pursuing Caesar's fleeing troops.

For the fact was that Pompey had, in a tactical sense, defeated his rival's army. What he failed to defeat, however, was Caesar's reputation. On the very verge of ultimate triumph, Pompey the Great was suddenly seized by the fear that he was about to fall into a trap. Like so many others who had gone up against Julius Caesar, Pompey believed that this vaunted military genius always had a trap prepared to snare the unwary. Giving in to his fear, Pompey abruptly broke off the pursuit, leaving Caesar, utterly amazed by his sudden deliverance, to remark, "The day was theirs had there been anyone among them to take it."

At Dyrrachium, Caesar, on the verge of a defeat that would have ended his career and, presumably, his life, found salvation not in the force of arms immediately available to him but in the compelling power of his reputation. Riding it, he lived to fight another day. Pompey's loss of nerve at Dyrrachium, which drove him to snatch defeat from the very jaws of victory, was certainly a boon to Caesar, but it was hardly a matter of dumb luck. For Caesar himself had built his reputation for victory. It was real. It was based on a mountain of fact. The record of past achievement Caesar had compiled defeated Pompey as surely as if he had been beaten by the army Caesar led.

Go ahead, ride your reputation and ride it as hard as you can. Just be certain you have created a reputation that can stand up to that hard riding. Good luck is almost certainly not enough.

■

Lesson 46
Know When to Be Caesar and Not to Be King

"No, I am Caesar, not King."

~Julius Caesar, quoted in Suetonius, *The Twelve Caesars*

On January 26, 44 BCE, Caesar, acclaimed dictator for life, was greeted by a crowd shouting to him *Rex! Rex!* (King! King!). He reportedly replied to the clamoring crowd, "No, I am Caesar, not King."

In part, this was a witticism. "Caesar" was the cognomen–the traditional Roman third name–that had been associated with the Julii Caesares, the family of Julius Caesar, since Numerius Julius Caesar, grandson of the first recorded member of the Julii clan, Lucius Julius Libo, who had been born sometime before 300 BCE. Because of Julius Caesar's martial and political deeds, the name began to take on the meaning that came to be applied to it regularly by about 68–69 CE, well after Julius Caesar's assassination: *emperor.* In 44 BCE, however, Caesar was clearly aware that his cognomen was already being used as a synonym for emperor or king–hence the wit of his reply to the crowd that would elevate him to *rex.*

The month after this exchange, on February 15, as Caesar presided over the Lupercalia, an ancient festival of communal purification and fertility honoring the god Pan, Cassius and Casca approached the new "dictator for life," who was seated as if on a throne, and laid a laurel crown on his knees. Apparently seeking to upstage the pair, the always impetuous Marc Antony snatched the crown and placed it on Caesar's head. Caesar quickly removed the diadem and tossed it into the crowd, exhorting them to dedicate it to the god Jupiter Capitolinus, whom he called "the only king in Rome."

Caesar understood that he already enjoyed absolute power—or at least the closest a citizen of the Roman Republic could get to it. He further grasped that his power flowed first and last from the acclaim of the people. Tossing the crown to them was no act of false modesty, but a powerful acknowledgment of the true source of his authority. In this relationship, Caesar believed, his power was far more secure than any hollow title could make it.

CEO, president, chairman, manager, director, supervisor, boss—there are many titles for leaders in business. All are words describing authority. None, however, are actual sources of authority. Leadership is conferred not by name, position, or high salary, but by the daily consent of those who agree to be led. Authority is a commodity given, not taken.

■

Tactics and Techniques

Lesson 47
Read the Landscape

> "For there was in that town an abundant supply of all things
> needful for war, and the place was so well fortified by Nature as to
> afford great facilities for the conduct of a campaign."
>
> ~Julius Caesar, *The Gallic War*, Book I

After he manipulated the defiant Suebi leader Ariovistus into inviting his attack so that he could expand his war of Roman conquest in Gaul, Caesar led his legions toward Vesontio on the Doubs River (the town of Besançon, in the Franche-Comté region of modern France). At the time, Vesontio was the largest town of the Sequani, the tribe Caesar had pledged to defend. He understood that the town was a key strategic prize because it offered "an abundant supply of all things needful for war" and was naturally sited so as "to afford great facilities for the conduct of a campaign." The Doubs River, Caesar further noted, "with a circuit that might have been traced by compasses, surrounds well-nigh the whole town." The "remaining space," he observed, "is closed in by a height of great eminence, so placed that its foundations touch the river-bank on either side. This height is surrounded by a wall to form a citadel and join it with the town."

In short, Vesontio was a natural fortress, a naturally commanding high ground, and Caesar's instant recognition of this fact is one of military history's greatest examples of a strategic and tactical ability military writers have traditionally called *coup d'oeil.* The phrase describes the faculty of a commander that allows him instantly, with a single glance (a "cut of the eye"), to understand and assess the advantages and vulnerabilities of a position to be contested, taken, defended, and held. In a flash, Caesar recognized

Vesontio as the single greatest prize in all the territory of the Sequani: stocked by man with the materials of war and fitted by nature as the ideal fortress. In a flash, Caesar identified his chief military objective in the campaign against Ariovistus.

> **Perfect the art of** the *coup d'oeil*. Learn to quickly and decisively assess the tactical and strategic landscape around you, to identify the principal strengths and key weaknesses, the assets and liabilities, the opportunities for leverage and the dangers of deficiencies and deficits. Use your assessment to formulate your priorities, objectives, and goals. Having done so, emulate Caesar in his advance on Vesontio, pushing "on with forced marches by night and day" to seize the prize before others, whose tactical and strategic glance may not be quite so fast or encompassing.

■

Lesson 48
Welcome Threat as Opportunity

> "Then accordingly he determined that he must no longer hesitate about moving against them. . . . He arrived . . . unexpectedly, and with more speed than anyone had looked for."
>
> ~Julius Caesar, *The Gallic War*, Book II

After defeating the Suebi warrior leader Ariovistus and his German tribal allies, Caesar rested his army in winter quarters in Cisalpine Gaul—roughly northern Italy, including what is today Emilia-Romagna, Friuli-Venezia Giulia, Liguria, Lombardy, Piedmont, Trentino-Alto Adige, and Veneto. While quartered here, he began to receive word of a new uprising, perpetrated by the Belgae, a confederation of tribes living in northern Gaul on the west bank of the Rhine. Collectively, they occupied about a third of the Gallic region. (The other two parts, according to Caesar, were inhabited by the Aquitani—or Celts—and the Galli.)

Caesar regarded the Belgae as militarily more formidable than even the Helvetii, and of the three major peoples of Gaul they were (in Caesar's estimation) "the most courageous, because they are farthest removed from the culture and civilization of the [Roman] Province, and least often visited by merchants introducing the commodities that make for effeminacy." Far from being intimidated by the Belgic threat, however, Caesar welcomed the opportunity to push Roman conquest yet farther into Gaul. Thus, instead of responding defensively to the rumors of uprising, he prevailed on his Gallic allies, especially the Senones, neighbors of the Belgae, to report to him in detail on their activities. When they informed him that "bands were being collected," Caesar "determined that he must no longer hesitate about moving against them."

Clearly, he was eager for a fight that would justify furthering his campaign of imperial conquest; nevertheless, he took care to secure his grain supply before striking camp and commencing his march eastward to the borders of the Belgae. Once he was confident that food stores were plentifully in place, he led a forced march that brought his legions to the Belgic threshold "unexpectedly" and with "more speed than anyone had looked for."

The speed of Caesar's advance was typical of his campaign tactics. He embraced challenge as opportunity. Then he harnessed that passion for conquest as the driver of decisive headlong speed, which he held to be indispensable to victory. At the same time, he never allowed the urgency of action to cause careless mistakes. Before launching his forces preemptively against the Belgae, Caesar took elaborate care to secure his army's sustenance. He knew that, while valor was indispensable to victory, an army could not survive on valor alone.

> **The philosopher-poet** Ralph Waldo Emerson wrote that "nothing great was ever achieved without enthusiasm." Caesar was a classic enthusiast, a leader whose passion is fired by challenge rather than dismayed by it. He cherished the fire in the belly, but he knew also that bellies had to be filled. Even as he embraced danger and launched his men directly into it, he made all prudent provisions for their survival and sustenance. Passion is no excuse for recklessness.

■

Lesson 49
Choose Your Battlefield

> "He chose a ground . . . naturally suitable and appropriate . . ."
> ~Julius Caesar, *The Gallic War*, Book II

After staging many modest cavalry probes against the Belgae (see Lesson 24, "Probe and Prove"), Caesar determined that his men "were not inferior" to this vaunted and much-dreaded foe, and he therefore decided to commit to a showdown battle against them.

As was at all times his practice, once he had made the decision to fight, Caesar seized the initiative by refusing to let the enemy choose the battleground. He identified and chose what he judged to be the ideal ground. It was a short distance from the Roman camp, which meant that his lines of communication and supply would be short and therefore readily defended, and that a place of fortified refuge would be available. The field also possessed an important natural advantage in that it was slightly elevated above the plain, offering "to the front as broad a space as a line deployed could occupy," but, to the sides—the ever-vulnerable flanks of the army—the ground "fell away" more sharply, thereby hindering an enemy flanking attack. The ground, therefore, naturally offered advantages for Caesar's own frontal attack against his adversary while simultaneously presenting obstacles to an enemy attack on his flanks.

For Caesar, what nature provided was always nothing more— and nothing less—than a starting point. He ordered his men to dig a "protecting trench" at right angles to the sharp slope on both of his flanks. At the ends of these projecting trenches, he "constructed forts and there posted his artillery, so that, when he had formed line, the enemy might not be able, because of their great superiority of numbers, to surround the Romans fighting on the flanks." In this way, Caesar amplified what nature provided.

Having chosen and embellished the battlefield, Caesar next deliberately provoked an attack by an enemy that relied heavily on its superiority in numbers. What the Belgae failed to take into their calculation, however, was that Caesar's choice of field and his improvements upon it had effectively neutralized much of the advantage of their greater numbers. The Belgae, therefore, entered the battle with a grossly inflated confidence that they would easily win an overwhelming victory. Nothing is more demoralizing than the sudden, stunning collapse of comfortable self-confidence.

The successful leader is, above all else, a successful manager. She manages every aspect of the situation into which she leads her enterprise, taking steps to increase advantages while simultaneously reducing dangers by both acquiring and leveraging assets while minimizing liabilities. As for the middle ground between advantage and disadvantage—call it chance—she works to convert as many random elements into favorable probabilities and, where possible, desirable certainties. This process of strategic and tactical management begins with the choice of "battlefield," which may mean (among many other things) a new market, a new territory, a new product line, or a promising technology. The choice must be conscious, deliberate, thoughtful, and always calculated to increase your advantages at the expense of your competition.

Lesson 50

Rally Your Centurions

> "He went forward into the first line, and, calling on the centurions by name, and cheering on the rank and file, he bade them advance."
>
> ~Julius Caesar, *The Gallic War*, Book II

Caesar put much trust in his subordinate generals, but the officers he most valued were the centurions. A Roman legion in Caesar's army consisted of ten cohorts, each of which was divided into six centuries. Theoretically, a century consisted of one hundred men—roughly the equivalent of a company in a modern U.S. infantry formation–although many centuries were actually smaller, consisting of fifty men, and some were larger, encompassing as many as two hundred, but most actually had eighty men. Regardless of the precise number of soldiers he commanded, the centurion was the primary operational officer in the field, the equivalent of a modern company captain.

Centurions rose in seniority within their cohort, their performance recognized by successive promotion to command of centuries that had earned through valor in combat higher precedence within the cohort. Ultimately, the senior-most centurion, as commander of the senior century, was effectively commander of the entire cohort. The very best senior centurions were elevated to centurions of the First Cohort. These men took command of one of the First Cohort's ten centuries and assumed a position on the staff of the legion's general. Within the legion, the top centurion was called the Primus Pilus, literally the "first spear," had command of the First Century of the First Cohort, and was therefore the lead legion commander directly under the legion's general.

Caesar carefully cultivated all the centurions within his army, personally praising and promoting all the standouts, thereby creating direct loyalty to himself within all of the ranks. With sixty centurions in a legion, and an army consisting of four, eight, or more legions, Caesar's ability to call upon the centurions by name—in the chaos of combat, no less—was an estimable achievement.

> **Caesar understood the critical** importance of the layer of command between himself and his soldiers: the centurions. He devoted much time and effort to cultivating, developing, improving, training, rewarding, and rallying them. The executive power of a chief *executive* officer is only theoretical until it is put into effective execution by the managers of the organization. Cultivate them, develop them, improve, train, and reward them. When the need comes, rally them—by name.

■

Lesson 51
Pitch In

> "His coming brought hope to the troops and renewed their spirit; each man of his own accord, in sight of the commander-in-chief, desperate as his own case might be, was fain to do his utmost. So the onslaught of the enemy was checked a little."
> ~Julius Caesar, *The Gallic War*, Book II

Overwhelmed by the onslaught of the Nervii, the fiercely warlike tribe of the northeastern hinterlands of Gaul, far from the moderating influences of anything approaching civilization, Caesar saw that the "condition of affairs" among his frightened and beleaguered troops "was critical indeed, and there was no support that could be sent up." His response in this potentially cataclysmic crisis was to pitch in bodily, throwing himself conspicuously into the front line of the battle. He took "a shield from a soldier of the rearmost ranks, as he himself was come thither without a shield" (that is how quickly he had come to the front) and, with it, "he went forward into the first line."

At first glance, it may be difficult to decide whether Caesar's act was very brave or very desperate and therefore foolhardy. But look beyond that first glance and consider closely Caesar's report of the battle.

He pitches in, but he takes care not to sacrifice himself impulsively. Although he rushed to the front, he does take the time to commandeer a shield before he advances into the first line. Once there, he calls "on the centurions by name." This means that he knows them, each of them, these front-line field commanders, and he wants to make certain that *they* know he knows them and that he is watching them.

Having rallied his officers, Caesar cheers "on the rank file," bidding "them advance"—*bidding,* not ordering. It is a request rather than a command—and even less a threat or ultimatum. Moreover, Caesar does not merely urge them forward, quite possibly to their deaths, but endeavors to get them to "extend the companies, that they might ply swords more easily"—that is, to maneuver so as to make sufficient room between them so that they might fight more effectively. He does not want them to die gloriously, but to fight effectively. His exhortation, therefore, is both an attempt to heighten morale and to give practical guidance in close-fighting tactics. The problem, he sees, is that, hemmed in by the enemy, his troops are bunched together too closely to fight effectively. Instead of furnishing empty cheers, he seeks to dispense a remedy for what is literally a tight situation.

Caesar's presence is not only of practical value, but works a motivational magic, bringing hope, a renewed sense of group cohesiveness, a willingness to sacrifice for the good of the organization, and a desire to perform heroically under the eyes of the commander-in-chief.

Get your hands dirty. Grab a wrench, a keyboard, a shield—whatever the tools of your trade—and pitch in. Show yourself. Reach out. Call people by their names. Encourage and inspire, but never stop observing. Going into cheerleader mode does not require you to suspend the nitty-gritty business of practical management. Rally your forces, but never stop solving problems.

Lesson 52
Confess Weakness and Learn to Be Strong

> "When our own fleet encountered these ships [of the Gauls and
> Celts] it proved its superiority only in speed and oarsmanship; in
> all other respects, having regard to the locality and force of the
> tempests, the others were more suitable and adaptable."
>
> ~Julius Caesar, *The Gallic War*, Book III

In 56 BCE, when Caesar commenced his campaign to put down the rebellion of the mighty Veneti of the Brittany peninsula and the tribes allied to them, he soon discovered that the Veneti towns were immensely difficult to attack or even to access. Caesar responded to the problem analytically. "The positions of the strongholds were generally of one kind," he wrote. "They were set at the end of tongues and promontories, so as to allow no approach on foot, when the tide rushed in from the sea—which regularly happens every twelve hours—nor in ships, because when the tide ebbed again the ships would be damaged in shoal water. Both circumstances, therefore, hindered the assault on the strongholds." If the Romans succeeded in bringing their siege towers close to a town's wall, the Veneti "would bring close inshore a large number of ships, of which they possessed an unlimited supply, and take off all their stuff and retire to the nearest strongholds, there to defend themselves again with the same advantages of position."

Throughout the summer of 56 BCE, the Veneti and their allies successfully "pursued these tactics," Caesar explained, "because our own ships were detained by foul weather, and because the difficulty of navigation on a vast and open sea, with strong tides and few—nay, scarcely any—harbours, was extreme."

Caesar did not intend this explanation to excuse his failure. He was not blaming the weather and the ocean. For he pointed out that the "ships of the Gauls" suffered from none of the difficulties that assailed the Roman craft. Why not? Caesar again resorted to rigorous analysis, describing both the flaws of the Roman ships and the virtues of the Gallic vessels, which were (he wrote) "built and equipped in the following fashion":

> Their keels were considerably more flat than those of our own ships, that they might more easily weather shoals and ebb-tide. Their prows were very lofty, and their sterns were similarly adapted to meet the force of waves and storms. The ships were made entirely of oak, to endure any violence and buffeting. The cross-pieces were beams a foot thick, fastened with iron nails as thick as a thumb. The anchors were attached by iron chains instead of cables.

Caesar continued by explaining the effect of the enemy shipwrights' use of "skins and pieces of leather finely finished" in place of conventional cloth sails. This substitution, he wrote, might have been made "because the natives had no supply of flax or no knowledge of its use," but (and here Caesar exercised unsparing honesty by refusing to assume that the Gauls and Celts were intellectually or technologically inferior to the Romans) "more probably, because they thought that the mighty ocean-storms and hurricanes could not be ridden out, nor the mighty burden of their ships conveniently controlled, by means of [cloth] sails."

If Caesar had any reluctance to concede Roman inferiority, he readily overcame it in analyzing the superiority of the Gallic vessels:

> When our own fleet encountered these ships it proved its superiority only in speed and oarsmanship; in all other respects, having regard to the locality and the force of the tempests, the others were more suitable and adaptable. For our ships could not damage them with the ram (they were so stoutly built), nor, by reason of their height, was it easy to hurl a pike, and for the same reason they were less readily gripped by grapnels. Moreover, when the wind began to rage and they ran before it, they endured the storm more easily, and rested in shoals more safely, with no fear of rocks or crags if

left by the tide; whereas our own vessels could not but dread the possibility of all these chances.

Faced with a demonstration of the shortcomings of oneself or one's organization, the natural tendency is to move in the direction of self-excuse or outright denial. Caesar successfully resisted this urge and instead kept his eyes wide open to the problems that revealed themselves in his early action against the Veneti. In taking this unblinking approach, he manifested a key principle of leadership and management. He recognized weakness, confessed the weakness, and analyzed the weakness, all the while learning what it would take to convert that weakness into strength. In later sea combat off the coast of Gaul, he would commission ships that emulated the best features of Gallic construction—a design better suited to the local weather, tides, and other conditions of that part of the world.

■

Lesson 53
Attack for Effect

> "And as all the hope of the Gallic ships lay in their sails and tackle, when these were torn away all chance of using their ships was taken away also."
>
> ~Julius Caesar, *The Gallic War*, Book III

Caesar was brutally honest in his assessment of the great superiority of the Gallic and Celtic ships over those he commanded (Lesson 52, "Confess Weakness and Learn to Be Strong"). His analysis revealed the inadequacy of the customary Roman naval weapons. The Gallic vessels withstood storms better than the Roman ships did, and their relatively shallow draft negotiated treacherous shoal waters with ease.

Yet anatomizing the inferiority of Roman naval architecture was not the ultimate purpose of Caesar's thorough and unblinking military analysis. That analysis also revealed that, for all their virtues, the superiority of the enemy's ships depended above all else on a single feature: "their sails and tackle." What the Gaul and Celt mariners saw as a great asset, Caesar recognized as a vulnerability—a liability. As he reasoned, if the sails and tackles could somehow be "torn away all chance of using their ships was taken away also."

Somehow. That was the question. By what means could the enemy's tackle and sails be torn away?

"One device our men had prepared to great advantage," Caesar reported. He then described "sharp-pointed hooks let in and fastened to long poles, in shape not unlike siege-hooks. When by these contrivances the halyards which fastened the yards to the masts [of the enemy ships] were caught and drawn taut, the [attacking Roman] ship was rowed hard ahead and they [the halyards] were snapped short. With the halyards cut, the yards of necessity fell down," and without yardarms to hold the sails, the sails were torn away, leaving the enemy ships dead in the water, unable to maneuver, helpless. The enemy's greatest advantage was thereby neutralized.

Self-criticism is an invaluable tactical and strategic instrument. Like any tool, it can be used poorly or skillfully. A self-critical analysis that serves only to tear down an inefficient, inadequate, or counterproductive set of concepts and procedures is but a half measure, literally and by definition destructive. You must take the next step. Having torn down, follow your analysis to build up. Dismantle the ineffective only if you can replace it with what is effective.

Caesar and his sailors understood the weakness of the Roman vessels and the strength of the enemy's. Proceeding from this understanding, Caesar's sailors fashioned a weapon that would allow them to attack for effect, depriving the enemy precisely of his source of strength and advantage. The analysis, painful though it might have been, was carried to completion, so that the rival's edge became not merely a source of anguish and frustration but a target for destruction.

■

Lesson 54
Always Play to Your Advantage

> "The rest of the conflict was a question of courage, in which our own troops easily had the advantage."
>
> ~Julius Caesar, *The Gallic War*, Book III

In the initial confrontation between the ships of the Veneti and those of Rome (Lesson 52, "Confess Weakness and Learn to Be Strong"), Caesar calmly analyzed the significant tactical superiority of the enemy ships. As a result of this analysis, he identified the principal source of their superiority and his men devised a means of attacking that source, thereby depriving the Veneti of their tactical edge (Lesson 53, "Attack for Effect"). Once the enemy's advantage had been neutralized, Caesar understood that it had become possible to play to the advantage of his troops.

That advantage, he wrote, was in courage, and it was amplified "because the engagement took place in sight of Caesar and of the whole army, so that no exploit a little more gallant than the rest could escape notice." That is, his men, naturally courageous, were put in a position that leveraged this natural advantage. They were motivated to maximum effort by the opportunity for glory. As Caesar narrated: "When the yards [yardarms suspending the sails of the enemy ships] had been torn down . . . and each [now disabled] ship . . . surrounded by two or three [Roman vessels], the troops strove with utmost force to climb onto the enemy's ships. When several of them had been boarded, the natives saw what was toward; and, as they could think of no device to meet it, they hastened to seek safety in flight." This in itself constituted their defeat, but then the wind died down and a "calm so complete and absolute came on that they could not stir from the spot." As a result, virtually all of the enemy ships were boarded and captured, very few reaching land.

> **Leverage your advantage** by reducing your rival's advantage. Work strength against weakness. Bring your best against the other side's worst.

■

Lesson 55
Build Better Ships

> "He set forth the plan and pattern of the new ships."
>
> ~Julius Caesar, *The Gallic War*, Book V

In ancient warfare—indeed, in warfare prior to the twentieth century—winter was generally shunned as a season for active campaigning and battle. For Caesar, however, this did not mean that winter was to be taken as a season for rest or idleness. He used the winter of 54 BCE to return, as was his custom, from Gaul to Italy, to renew his contact with the centers of Roman political power (see Lesson 74, "Go Back to Italy"), but he "ordered the lieutenant-generals in charge of the legions to have as many ships as possible built during the winter," so that they would be prepared for the renewed major campaigns of spring.

The new ships he ordered were not to be vessels of the traditional Roman design that had proved inferior to the vessels of the Veneti in the campaigning of 56 BCE (see Lesson 52, "Confess Weakness and Learn to Be Strong"). Having observed two years earlier how brilliantly Veneti shipwrights had adapted their naval designs to the conditions that prevailed along their coasts, Caesar personally "set forth the plan and pattern of the new ships." Caesar's required specifications embodied a combination of lessons learned from the Veneti and innovations apparently of his own making.

Caesar understood that his vessels were to be used, first and foremost, for amphibious warfare; therefore he designed them not for long-haul ocean voyaging (as Roman ships typically were fashioned), but rather for "speed of loading and for purposes of beaching." This meant building them "somewhat lower that those which we are accustomed to use on our own [Mediterranean] sea." The lower profile was also the result of lessons learned from the humiliating Roman experience against the Veneti ships. The lower design, with its shallower draft, was far better adapted to the coastal waters of Gaul, where, Caesar now knew, "the turns of the tides" were more frequent and the waves "generally smaller" than they were along the Mediterranean coasts so familiar to Romans.

Caesar further decided that his ships had to be built to transport the large amounts of cargo that were necessary to support armies of invasion and occupation. "For the transport of cargo, and of the numerous draught-animals," therefore, he ordered "ships somewhat broader [in the beam] than those we use on the other seas." Moreover, all "of them he ordered to be fitted for oars as well as sails, to which end their lowness of build helped much." For Caesar had learned the importance of speed and maneuverability close to shore—something relying on sails and wind power alone could not ensure.

Having experienced the superiority of Gallic ship design in the waters off the coast of Gaul, Caesar easily swallowed any Roman pride he may have felt and refused to insist, in defiance of the facts, on the superiority of Roman traditions of naval architecture. Instead, he both understood and accepted that

Roman ships were designed for the waters most familiar to Roman mariners, and because he obviously could not change the conditions of the Gallic seas to suit the Roman ships, he needed to change the ships—even if this meant radically altering the comfortable and the familiar.

Never make a fetish of tradition and policy. Design plant, procedures, and policies not only to accommodate the dynamic realities in which you operate, but to take full competitive advantage of them. The objective of enterprising leadership must never be to impose your concepts and methods on a given environment, but to create concepts and methods that make effective use of the realities of that environment to advance your organization within it.

■

Lesson 56
Leverage the "Readiness of Men to Believe What They Wish"

> "For while the temper of the Gauls is eager and ready to undertake a campaign, their purpose is feeble and in no way steadfast to endure disasters."
>
> ~Julius Caesar, *The Gallic War*, Book III

One of Caesar's commanders in the campaign against the Veneti of Brittany was Quintus Titurius Sabinus, who was now responsible for conducting a campaign against the Venelli (or Unelli) under the leadership of Viridovix in what is today the region south of modern Cherbourg, Normandy. Viridovix had supplemented his warriors with a large army recruited from neighboring tribes, especially the Lexovii, Curiosolitae, and Aulerci-Eburovices, as well as assorted mercenaries and brigands.

Titurius fully understood that it was his mission to restore Roman order in the region by suppressing Viridovix, but he was by nature and reputation a cautious commander uneager for pitched battle. In this instance, he apparently consciously decided to exploit his own reputation, which was widely known, even to the Gauls. He therefore kept his troops close to his camp, a circumstance that prompted Viridovix to establish his own encampment just two miles away. Virtually every day, Viridovix would send his warriors to form up just outside the Roman camp and taunt the troops. Titurius so consistently refused to take up the challenge that his own officers and men grumbled, clearly feeling deep shame.

As days and weeks passed, Titurius observed that Viridovix was growing increasingly careless. Titurius bribed one of the Roman-allied Gauls attached to his forces to feign desertion, call upon Viridovix, and "set before [him] the timidity of the Romans" as well as report to him that "Caesar himself was in straits and hard pressed by the Veneti." The bogus deserter was also to ratchet up his campaign of disinformation with a tale that Titurius was just about "to lead his army secretly out of his camp and . . . set out to the assistance of Caesar." Once delivered, this piece of news incited Viridovix's followers to cry "with one consent that the chance of successful achievement should not be lost." They clamored for an immediate attack on the Roman camp. "Many considerations encouraged the Gauls to this course," Caesar wrote, then catalogued them: "the hesitation of Sabinus [Titurius] during the previous days, the confirmation given by the deserter, the lack of victuals (for which they had made too careless a provision), the hope inspired by the Venetian war, and"–last but far from least–"the general readiness of men to believe what they wish." His commanders pressed Viridovix, who reluctantly authorized the attack on the Roman camp.

"Rejoicing at the permission given as though at victory assured," the Gallic warriors "collected faggots and brushwood to fill up the trenches of the Romans and marched on the camp."

Loaded down as they were with this heavy material, the Gauls "hastened at great speed" up to the Roman camp, which was located "on high ground, with a gradual slope from the bottom of about a mile." The determined rapidity of their advance and the burden they carried exhausted the attackers who "arrived out of breath." Seeing their depleted condition, Titurius "exhorted his troops, and gave the signal which they longed for. The enemy were hampered by reason of the burdens which they were carrying, and he [Titurius] ordered a sudden sortie to be made from two gates. The order was executed with the advantage of ground"–that is, the significant advantage of making a *downhill* attack on a tired enemy that labored *uphill*. The blithely over-confident attackers "were inexperienced and fatigued," whereas the Romans were "courageous and schooled by previous engagements. The result was that without standing even one of our attacks the Gauls immediately turned and ran."

The Roman infantry and cavalry pursued the routed Gauls, slaughtering most of them. Legion infantrymen and cavalry followed hard at their heels, slaughtering the greater part of them. This defeat, coupled with the freshly arrived news of Caesar's triumph over the fleet of the mighty Veneti (Lesson 54, "Always Play to Your Advantage"), instantly brought the entire region into full submission to Rome.

A competent leader copes with reality as it is. An exceptional leader shapes reality to suit his purposes. In the case of the boldest of leaders—men like Alexander the Great, Hannibal, Caesar, and Napoleon—great fortresses were built, monumental sieges conducted, mighty rivers were bridged, and lofty mountains crossed. The very physical contours of the earth were altered. But even leaders of somewhat more modest stamp, such as Quintus Titurius Sabinus, took steps to alter the perception of reality, if not reality itself.

Create and manage image and expectation, play upon the natural "readiness of men to believe what they wish," and you may be able to paint a picture of circumstances precisely fitted to your objectives and goals just as effectively as if you had it within your power to alter the physical contours of reality itself.

■

Lesson 57
An Exemplary Campaign

> "Upon hearing of this battle the greatest part of Aquitania surrendered to Crassus, and of its own motion sent hostages, among whom were representatives of the Tarbelli, Bigerriones, Ptianii, Vocates, Tarusates, Elusates, Gates, Ausci, Graumni, Sibuzates, Cocosates."
>
> ~Julius Caesar, *The Gallic War*, Book III

There can be no denying that Julius Caesar composed his history of the conquest of Gaul chiefly to celebrate his own intrepid military genius with the aim of embellishing and adding to the glory necessary to fuel any rise to power in the Roman world. This said, Caesar was also generous in his careful documentation and sincere celebration of the victories of his lieutenants, among whom was Marcus Licinius Crassus, who commanded the Roman legions in Gallia Aquitania, the region that is now Aquitaine in southwestern France. Here, not many years before, the forces of Rome had suffered a stunning defeat. Crassus more than redeemed this humiliation and, what is more, did so in a manner so exemplary that Caesar devoted particular care in narrating it.

It is clear from Caesar's history of the Gallic War that he believed the most instructive portion of the campaign came when Crassus arrayed his outnumbered forces in a double line, fully prepared for battle, then, practicing great restraint, patiently "waited to see what plan the enemy would adopt." Crassus understood the advantage of letting the enemy tip his hand and commit to a course of action, to which a skilled commander could respond by adopting an approach precisely calculated to defeat it. According to Caesar's account, Crassus concluded that the Gauls "considered that they could fight an action safely by reason of their numbers and their past glory in war and the smallness of the Roman force." Nevertheless, as Crassus observed, "they still thought it safer to close the roads and cut off supplies, and so to secure victory without bloodshed." Seeing this, Crassus was able to assume that the enemy commanders suffered from timidity, and timidity created a great vulnerability that he intended to exploit. What is more, Crassus also recognized the effect of this apparent timidity on his own soldiers, whose eagerness for action was increased and resulted in "a general protest . . . against longer delay before an advance on the [enemy] camp." Seizing on their "general enthusiasm," Crassus "harangued his troops" and "pressed on to the enemy's camp."

Once arrived before the enemy camp, Crassus assigned some men to "fill up the trenches" while "others by many volleys of missiles [cleared] the defenders from the rampart and fortifications." Simultaneously, he assigned his auxiliaries, "in whom [he] had no great confidence for actual fighting," to such labor and support duties as handing up ammunition and "carrying sods to make a [siege] ramp"; however, even as he set them to work in this manner, he was careful to order them to maintain the *appearance* of being combat troops, so as to give the impression to the enemy that they were confronting a 100 percent frontline fighting force.

The enemy, however, proved to be no pushover. They fought, Caesar records, "in no irresolute or cowardly fashion, and their missiles discharged from a higher level fell to some purpose." Nevertheless, Crassus skillfully deployed his cavalry to probe the full extent of the enemy's defenses, and, "having moved round the enemy's camp, [they] reported to Crassus that it was not fortified with the same care on the rear side, and might easily be approached there."

Acting on this intelligence, Crassus focused his attack and exhorted his "cavalry commanders to incite their men by great rewards and promises" to lead "out the cohorts which had been left to guard the camp and were unwearied by exertion" by taking them the long way around, "so as not to be seen from the enemy's camp." They were then to lead an assault on the camp via its poorly fortified rear. The Romans "threw down the fortifications, and established themselves in the enemy's camp before they could be clearly seen by them or their action perceived." Once they were discovered, however, and "shouting was heard," the rest of Crassus's forces, which had been engaged at the front of the camp, fought with "strength renewed . . . as is frequent and usual where there is hope of victory." The result was an enemy that suddenly found itself "surrounded on all sides and in utter despair." Instantly demoralized, they "hastened to lower themselves over the fortifications and to seek safety in flight." The Roman cavalry "chased them over plains wholly without shelter, and of fifty thousand . . . [the enemy] had left scarce a quarter when they returned to camp late at night." Word of the battle spread throughout the region, whereupon "the greatest part of Aquitania surrendered to Crassus" and thereby to Rome.

Caesar presents the campaign of Crassus in Aquitania as a kind of textbook model of applied tactics. Crassus prepares for combat but waits for the enemy to tip his hand. Discovering the foe's fatal flaw—timidity—Crassus proceeds accordingly, stirring his troops who are already eager for a fight. Laying siege to the enemy camp, Crassus is careful to assign his best combat troops to the most arduous combat assignments while reserving auxiliary forces for labor and support duty—yet, in so doing, ordering them to present the appearance of combat forces in order to intimidate the enemy.

Crassus does not simply slug it out against a fortified enemy. Instead, while the siege is under way, he uses his most mobile forces—his cavalry—for the role to which they are best suited: reconnaissance. They soon report a weak point in the enemy's fortifications, which Crassus is quick to exploit. Experience has taught this veteran commander that once any portion of his army makes a breakthrough, the entire army will be energized by the hope of victory (the "frequent and usual" outcome of such a hope), so that the breakthrough at the enemy's rear is quickly leveraged into a general breakthrough that surrounds and overruns the camp, and which sends the enemy into panic and rout. No army is more vulnerable than when it is in disorderly retreat, and Crassus wastes no time in pursuing the enemy to its destruction.

Study every example of successful strategy and tactics you can find. Don't just admire what you see. Deconstruct it. Reverse-engineer it. Understand it. Prepare yourself to adapt and emulate it.

■

Lesson 58
Choose a Safe Landing

> "He gave the signal, and weighed anchor, and, moving on about seven miles from that spot, he grounded his ships where the shore was even and open."
>
> ~Julius Caesar, *The Gallic War*, Book IV

Caesar seems to have truly burned to explore Britain. Even many otherwise admiring historians have criticized him as headstrong in his willingness to invade a remote island about which he knew so very little. There is no question that Caesar was by nature and habit a bold commander, and he never acted more boldly than in his decision to probe the wild country across the English Channel. What many historians do not give him sufficient credit for is that, even in his eagerness to get to Britain, he tempered boldness with prudence.

He reached the island "about the fourth hour of the day, and there beheld the armed forces of the enemy displayed on all the cliffs." The description has prompted scholars to speculate that Caesar's first anchorage was between Walmer and Deal, a landscape that presented a danger Caesar clearly perceived: "Such was the nature of the ground, so steep the heights which banked the sea, that a missile could be hurled from the higher levels onto the shore." He quickly decided that "this place [was] by no means suitable for disembarkation." After waiting at anchor "till the ninth hour for the rest of the flotilla to assemble [around him], Caesar ordered all vessels to sail southwest along the coast. When they reached the vicinity of modern Dover, "where the shore was even and open," Caesar finally disembarked his men.

There is no reward without risk, but thoughtless repetition of this mantra does not excuse you from evaluating and managing the risk. Faced with a hostile array of tribesmen, Caesar did not turn back from Britain to the Continent. He did, however, continue to sail until he saw what he judged to be a safer landing place.

■

Lesson 59

Learn from Your Rivals

> "Thus they show in action the mobility of cavalry and the stability of infantry."
>
> ~Julius Caesar, *The Gallic War*, Book IV

In Britain, finding himself up against an enemy extraordinarily skilled in chariot tactics, Caesar chose as usual to learn from the enemy's demonstration of special skill rather than allow panic to blind him to it. His description of the action of the British charioteers might have been the work of some ancient author of a military textbook rather than what it was, the firsthand narrative of a desperate battle. Caesar calmly described how the British charioteers "drive in all directions and hurl missiles," so that "by the mere terror that the teams inspire and by the noise of the wheels they generally throw ranks into confusion."

Caesar's narrative treatment of the action is not merely descriptive, but, characteristically of the author, precisely analytical. After the two-man chariot teams had created panic, they would work "their way in between the troops of [Roman] cavalry" and the spear-throwers would "leap down from the chariots to fight on foot" while the chariot drivers (the troops who actually handle the horses) would "retire gradually from the combat, and dispose the chariots in such fashion that, if the warriors are hard pressed by the host of the enemy, they may have a ready means of retirement to their own side." Caesar clearly understood the great significance of this tactic, which gave the Britons the seemingly impossible: "the mobility of cavalry and the stability of infantry."

Caesar penetrated even more deeply into British chariot doctrine, observing that "by daily use and practice they become so accomplished that they are ready to gallop their teams down the steepest of slopes without loss of control, to check and turn them in a moment, to run along the pole, stand on the yoke, and then, quick as lightning, to dart back into the chariot."

> **Never turn away from** threat or adversity. Learn from it. Copy the best your adversaries and competition have to offer. Never stop looking, examining, analyzing, thinking. Salvage good ideas even from defeat.

■

Lesson 60
Form a Square

> "The Romans formed a square and defended themselves, and . . . some six thousand men speedily came about them [to attack]. Upon report of this Caesar sent the whole of the cavalry from the camp to assist his men. Meanwhile our troops withstood the enemy's assault, and fought with the greatest gallantry for more than four hours; they received but a few wounds, and slew a good many of the enemy."
>
> ~Julius Caesar, *The Gallic War*, Book IV

After withdrawing for a time from Britain and returning to Gaul, a detachment of Caesar's forces was attacked by "the Morini, who had been left by Caesar in a state of peace when he set out for Britain." Outnumbered by the warriors of this Belgic tribe who lived in the vicinity of modern Boulogne and Pas de Calais, the Romans responded to their demand to "lay down their arms if they did not wish to be killed" by forming a square. This was not only one of the most important elements in the Roman tactical vocabulary, it was a formation that endured into and beyond the Napoleonic era, well into the nineteenth century. It was something the men of the Roman legions drilled and practiced to perfection—an item of repertoire a commander could reliably summon up with a single order.

In response to the command *agmen formate*, the soldiers arranged themselves into a hollow square, each side of which was composed of two or more ranks of legionaries. The commander

[145]

and reserve forces were gathered in the center of the square. The advantages of this formation included a 360-degree defensive perimeter, which could fend off an attack coming from any direction; flexibility, which allowed troops to be quickly moved to reinforce whatever side of the square was absorbing the brunt of an attack at a given moment; protection of command and reserves, which were surrounded and protected by defensive troops; and a combination of stability and mobility: the square was a kind of portable fortress, its human "walls" resistant against attackers, yet, because the walls were human, easily moved from place to place.

There was one additional great advantage of the square: It was always ready. As a standard, well rehearsed, thoroughly drilled tactic, it did not have to be invented or improvised in an emergency; it just had to be called upon. It was an off-the-shelf solution to the most urgent of problems.

The effectiveness of the square against the attack of the Morini proved its great utility. The formation bought the outnumbered legionaries the precious time they needed to receive reinforcements, and it also cost the attackers many casualties. When the reinforcements finally arrived, the Morini, already demoralized by the Roman resistance, "threw down their arms and fled, and a great number of them were slain."

Spontaneity and improvisation are overrated assets in business. It is far better to develop a thoughtful and thoroughly vetted vocabulary of tactics, tweak and hone them continually, rehearse them to flawless perfection, then apply them—off the shelf, as it were—as the situation demands. Just make certain that the standard tactics you choose have, like the Roman square, stood the test of time and proven themselves consistently reliable and effective.

■

Lesson 61
Grow Tireless Legs

> "[Caesar] always exploited the dismay caused by his speed of execution and the fear engendered by his daring, rather than the strength created by his preparations."
>
> ~Appian of Alexandria (ca. 95–ca. 165 CE), *Civil Wars*, quoted in Nic Fields, *Julius Caesar: Leadership, Strategy, Conflict* (2010)

Caesar rarely enjoyed superiority of numbers in any of the battles he fought. Over and over again, he relied instead on speed—speed of movement from place to place as well as speed of maneuver and tactical execution once the battle had been joined. The Roman historian Suetonius wrote that Caesar engaged in a battle "not only after planning his movements beforehand but also on the spur of the moment." What is more, not only would he move and execute quickly, but "often at the end of a march, and sometimes in miserable weather, when he would be least expected to make a move." As military historian Nic Fields put it, for Caesar, "speed of foot replaced numbers of men," and the "secret of his success was in his tireless legs."

The British historian J. F. C. Fuller explained in his 1965 book *Julius Caesar: Man, Soldier and Tyrant*, that Caesar departed from the accepted military doctrine of his day by basing his operations on speed and audacity rather than on a preponderance of superior numbers. Had he access to unlimited resources, so that he could have assembled much larger armies, one wonders if he would have been so consistently victorious.

Caesar learned to make a virtue of smallness—small units could move faster, perform more flexibly, and be more responsive to commands than large armies. Create efficiency, cultivate flexibility, move quickly, create surprise. Grow tireless legs.

■

[147]

Lesson 62
Convert, Don't Kill, Your Enemies

> "Do you see what kind of man we are dealing with? He has moved against the Republic with such cleverness, such care, such preparation. I truly believe that if he continues to spare all lives and property he will convert his most bitter enemies into ardent supporters."
>
> ~ Cicero, *Letters to Atticus*

Lucius Domitius Ahenobarbus had long been a jealous rival of Caesar and, in the Civil War, took it upon himself, independently of both the Senate and Pompey, to defeat his personal enemy. He sought to check Caesar's advance against Rome at Corfinium (near modern Corfinio in Italy's Abruzzo), just about a hundred miles east of the Roman capital, but soon found himself hopelessly surrounded and besieged. Domitius was thrown into such a panic that he called on his personal physician to prepare a poison for him to swallow, lest he fall into Caesar's unforgiving hands alive. The medical man gave him the requested potion, Domitius impulsively drank it down—then thought the better of it. Perhaps he should just try to escape or even risk surrender. When he asked if there was an antidote, his doctor answered that, anticipating precisely this change of heart, he had not actually put any poison in the drink.

Thus reprieved, Domitius decided to take flight. Unfortunately for him, his subordinates overheard his plans and, rather than die in battle against Caesar after being deserted by their commander, they arrested Domitius and dispatched a message to Caesar, offering to surrender and yield their erstwhile commander to him.

Caesar did nothing until the next morning, when Domitius, together with an assortment of senators, equestrians (knights), and tribunes who had chosen to follow him, trooped fearfully into Caesar's camp. They anticipated nothing less than death. If they were lucky, it would be swift. If unlucky, slow and very painful.

Caesar met them, looked them up and down, and then spoke to them. He neither condemned nor cursed these men who had so earnestly sought his destruction. Instead, he told them that they should have behaved better. With that, he ordered them to be set free. Domitius had brought with him a stash of treasure—his army's payroll. Though he badly needed money to finance his own military campaigning, Caesar told Domitius to take the treasure with him. He wanted to demonstrate to Rome that he was no pirate, plunderer, or thief.

The news of Caesar's unexpected magnanimity swept through Rome with far greater effect than if it had been a gory account of the bloodiest revenge. Caesar had anticipated and intended his mercy to make just such a public relations impact. For his part, Cicero, on the side of Pompey and the Optimates, was puzzled, marveling to his closest friend, Titus Pomponius Atticus, that such kindness would "convert [Caesar's] most bitter enemies into ardent supporters."

Caesar knew he could not kill everyone who opposed him, so he endeavored instead, whenever possible, to convert enemies into allies.

The world of business, especially within the confines of a given industry or even a particular company, is far smaller than the world of Caesar's Rome. You cannot kill everyone who opposes you, and you can be certain that you will encounter and deal with the same people over and over again. Therefore, don't slam the door on anyone, no matter how unfriendly they may be. Instead, give them the best reasons you can to enter your office as colleagues, allies, and ardent supporters.

■

Lesson 63
Woo Your Enemy

> "I especially hope to see you when I return to Rome. I'm in great need of your help and sage advice, being the popular and influential man you are."
>
> ~Julius Caesar to Cicero, quoted in Cicero, *Letters to Atticus*

As the Civil War developed, Caesar did his best to woo Cicero from the camp of Pompey and the Optimates. As he marched toward Rome, he wrote him a flattering letter, asking for his "help and sage advice." For his part, Cicero was growing receptive, especially after marveling at Caesar's generous restraint against Domitius at Corfinium (see Lesson 62, "Convert, Don't Kill, Your Enemies"). When Caesar heard that his act of mercy had impressed Cicero, he wrote to assure him that "cruel revenge" was indeed the farthest thing from his mind. "Since mercy is so dear to me," he continued, "I'm glad that you support me in this. It doesn't bother me that those I released are fighting against me again. All I want is for every man to follow his own conscience."

The final sentence, concerning conscience, was precisely calculated to impress a noble political philosopher like Cicero, and he readily agreed to meet with Caesar. Flushed with success, Caesar called on him—only to be told by Cicero that his only viable course was to end his war with Pompey and submit himself to the authority of the Senate. Caesar politely declined, and after the two parted—civilly if not amicably—Cicero made his choice. He declared himself against Caesar and for Pompey in the belief that he, despite his many flaws, had the best prospects for preserving the Roman Republic.

Caesar's attempt to woo his enemy Cicero ultimately failed. This does not mean, however, that it had not been worthwhile. You build your influence—and therefore your power—on those whose support you win, not on those whose opposition you earn.

Lesson 64
Mature the Enterprise

> "For his services to himself and to the republic Caesar, having presented him with two hundred thousand sesterces and eulogized him, announced that he transferred [the centurion Scaeva] from the eighth cohort to the post of first centurion of the first cohort."
>
> ~Julius Caesar, *Civil Wars*, Book III

The Battle of Dyrrachium (at Durrës in modern Albania), fought in July of 48 BCE, was indecisive but is generally regarded as a victory for Pompey. Costly as it was for Caesar, he not only preserved his army as a result of the battle, but put it in position to deliver a decisive defeat against Pompey the Great at Pharsalus the following month.

Dyrrachium, Caesar writes, was actually a combination of six battles in a single day, July 10, 48 BCE, three at the town of Dyrrachium itself and three "at the outworks." In the "redoubt," a strongpoint fiercely defended by Caesar, casualties were very heavy. There was "not a single one of the men who was not wounded, and four centurions out of one cohort lost their eyes. . . . Wishing to produce a proof of their labour and peril, they counted out to Caesar about thirty thousand arrows which had been discharged at the redoubt, and when the shield of the centurion Scaeva was brought to him one hundred and twenty holes were found in it." Persuaded by this evidence that the "redoubt had been to a great extent preserved by [Scaeva's] aid," Caesar rewarded him with money, praise, and a spectacular promotion from command of a century in the eighth cohort (that is, the cohort eighth in seniority within the legion) to "the post of first centurion of the first cohort," essentially giving him the senior command of the legion under its legate (general).

Scaeva's promotion was not only a reward for a deserving individual, it was a way of ensuring that the best field commanders would lead the most men, for the *primus pilus* (the "first spear," the first centurion), exercised far more influence than a centurion back in the eighth cohort. Caesar consistently strengthened his legions by maturing them. He identified the best commanders and gave them the greatest responsibility. He also promoted veteran troops from veteran legions to higher positions in newly recruited legions, seeking to leaven rookie units with a strong presence of senior soldiers. In this way, he built a consistently formidable army.

> **Avoid creating elite units** at the expense of other units within your organization. Develop the entire enterprise. Mature the organization by infusing every unit with managers of proven merit and experienced staff. Cross-promote your most promising people, increasing their responsibility by moving them up, when possible and necessary, from a lower position in one unit to a higher position in another. Build a consistently formidable enterprise.

Lesson 65
Choose Quality over Quantity Every Time

> "When the Pompeians were driven in flight within the rampart, Caesar, thinking that no respite should be given them in their terror, urged his men to . . . attack the camp. And though fatigued by the great heat, for the action had been prolonged till noon, they nevertheless obeyed his command, with a spirit ready for every toil."
> ~Julius Caesar, *Civil Wars*, Book III

For his victory over his rival Pompey the Great at the Battle of Pharsalus on August 9, 48 BCE, Caesar credited the quality—the experience, the endurance, the courage, the spirit, and the loyalty—of his troops. As was most often the case in his battles, he was

[152]

significantly outnumbered, in this instance about two to one. But he believed that the quality of his soldiers more than balanced the disparity in quantity. To use a modern military term, quality was a "force multiplier," and, in this case, Caesar felt confident that quality would multiply his force by at least a factor of two.

It was not a mere guess or even less a hollow hope. He saw that the troops defending the rampart of Pompey's camp were in a panic. This state presented not only an opportunity for a breakthrough, but betrayed a deficiency in the overall quality of Pompey's force. A well fortified encampment of superior numbers should feel absolute confidence, not abject terror.

Once Caesar had succeeded in overrunning the camp, he saw ample evidence to confirm his analysis: "In the camp of Pompeius one might see bowers constructed, a great weight of silver plate set out, soldiers' huts laid with freshly cut turf, and those of Lucius Lentulus and some others covered over with ivy, and many other indications of excessive luxury and confidence of victory." Whereas Caesar's men, outnumbered and exhausted as they were, found the resources within themselves to obey their commander and, what is more, to do so with "a spirit ready for every toil," Pompey's overconfident troops had gone soft. The great advantage of their numbers was simply cancelled out.

Victories of small forces over large are rare in military history. We read about them precisely because they are remarkable, and so they are well known in history. Nevertheless, given troops more or less equally matched in quality and commanded by equally competent officers, the side with more men is more likely by far to prevail. However, in those instances in which the smaller force has significantly better troops and at least equally competent command, the advantage almost always goes to the side with the greater quality.

Quality is leverage. Invest in it, develop it, reward it.

Communication and Motivation

Lesson 66
Communicate Vividly and Effectively

> "Avoid an unfamiliar word as a sailor avoids the rocks."
> ~Julius Caesar, quoted by the grammarian Aulus Gellius
> (ca. 125–ca. 180 CE) in his commonplace book, *Attic Nights*

Caesar's two military histories, *The Gallic War* and *Civil Wars*, are universally considered masterpieces of classical literature. Unlike most literary works, which tend toward complexity, their great glory is their simplicity and directness. Anton Powell and Kathryn Welch, the editors of *Julius Caesar as Artful Reporter: The War Commentaries as Political Instruments* (1998), analyzed both works and calculated that Caesar employed a remarkably lean vocabulary of only 1,300 words, avoiding colloquialisms as well as foreign borrowings. Wielded by a lesser writer, this limited palette would quickly become monotonous. Caesar uses it vividly, and its straightforward economy of expression does much to convey a sense of objectivity, which is indispensable to a historical report.

The aura of reliably objective reporting Caesar projects in his military accounts is intensified by his use of the third person throughout both. The conventional rationale for referring to oneself in the third person is to avoid the apparent egotism of repeatedly using first-person pronouns. Brilliantly, however, by using the third person, Caesar adopts the convention of modesty while simultaneously putting himself in the position of broadcasting his name over and over. Powell and Welch count 775 repetitions of "Caesar" in *The Gallic War* and *Civil Wars,* prompting one historian—Nic Fields, in *Julius Caesar: Leadership, Strategy, Conflict* (2010)—to describe this strategy of repetition as a classical instance of what we would today call creating a "brand."

In communicating to those he needed to impress in Rome as well as to all history, Caesar branded himself as the go-to leader of victory and producer of empire. The makers of Stella Artois beer lay claim to having the world's oldest trademark, in continuous use since 1366. Caesar beat that brewer by some fourteen hundred years.

Make history. Present your work, your creations, your achievements vividly, succinctly, and persuasively. Account for accomplishments in actions and dollars, causes and effects, nouns and verbs. Avoid adjectives and adverbs. Let what you have done speak for itself in the most concrete and direct language possible. In this way, you will promote, not merely puff, yourself and, in the process, fashion a brand. Most historians are agreed that Julius Caesar was a military genius. How do they know his military achievements? Chiefly through his own writing.

■

Lesson 67
Refuse Victimhood

> "[Caesar] held them [his pirate captors] in such disdain that whenever he lay down to sleep he would send and order them to stop talking. For thirty-eight days, as if the men were not his watchers, but his royal bodyguard, he shared in their sports and exercises with great unconcern."
>
> ~Plutarch, *Life of Caesar*

In 75 BCE, young Julius Caesar, determined to perfect his command of persuasive oratory and rhetoric, embarked on a voyage across the Aegean Sea to Rhodes, where he planned to study with the great rhetorician Apollonius Molon. En route, near the island of Pharmacussa off the Asia Minor coast, his ship was captured by pirates. They instantly recognized Caesar as a Roman patrician and therefore announced their intention to hold him for a ransom of 20 silver talents—a lordly sum. At this, Caesar reportedly became incensed, proclaiming himself worth no less than 50 talents, which he pledged to pay them personally. He then dispatched his traveling companions to various destinations with instructions to obtain the loans necessary to raise the money.

A captive, Caesar refused to play the part of the captive. Everyone knows that kidnappers, not their victim, set the amount of a ransom. Caesar doubtless knew this as well, but nevertheless refused to concede to his kidnappers their customary role. Instead, he began his captivity by turning the tables and seizing control from them. For the next thirty-eight days, until he was ransomed, Caesar treated his captors alternately as his servants (worthy of "disdain"), as his personal bodyguards, as his playmates in sport, and as his audience for the "poems and sundry speeches" Plutarch says that he wrote and "read aloud to them." When some failed to admire his literary productions, Caesar "would call [them] to their faces illiterate Barbarians, and often laughingly threatened to hang them all." For their part, the "pirates were delighted at this, and attributed his boldness of speech to a certain simplicity and boyish mirth."

By refusing to play the role of victim—a part imposed on him by others—Caesar secured his safety and transformed what might have been a painful captivity into something that seems to have resembled a vacation. After his companions collected and delivered the ransom, Caesar was released and immediately sailed to the city of Miletus, on the west coast of Anatolia (the present-day Aydin Province of Turkey). Here he continued to refuse playing his "proper" role—that of the grateful ransomed captive—and instead persuaded local officials to muster a flotilla of warships and the crews to sail them, to put these under his command, and to send him on a mission to punish the pirates who had captured him. We do not know just how Caesar made his persuasive case to the officials of Miletus, but we can safely assume that whatever he said was indeed remarkable. For, at the time, Julius Caesar was just twenty-five, held no military or elective office, and had neither more nor less special authority than any other private citizen of Rome. As for the mission, Caesar sailed, landed precisely where he had been held prisoner, found the pirates still there, took *them* captive, and reclaimed not only his 50 talents, but also appropriated all of the booty they had acquired in the course of their piracy. Caesar transported his prisoners to Pergamum (modern Bakirçay, Turkey), and demanded of the local Roman governor, the propraetor Marcus Iuncus, that he execute them as pirates.

Apparently, Marcus Iuncus was far more interested in selling the pirates as slaves and pocketing the proceeds; he therefore refused to execute them. Now Caesar yet again declined to take on a role defined by others—in this case, the role of law-abiding Roman citizen. Bypassing the governor altogether, he personally ordered the pirates' jailers to crucify the prisoners. He had no legal authority to issue such an order, but the jailers asked no questions, and the pirates were duly crucified—just as Caesar had "laughingly threatened" during his captivity.

It's variously called brass, nerve, guts, bravado, temerity, chutzpah, and sometimes just plain *balls*. But what it really is, this quality of ultimate and utterly egocentric assertiveness, is an absolute unwillingness to meekly play the roles others would thrust upon us. The capacity for this refusal is a hallmark of the leadership personality, and it is a form of communication by which the leader persistently defines himself or herself in his or her own terms.

Fail to define yourself, and others will surely define you—almost always to your disadvantage. Fail to define yourself, and you risk being defined, by default, as a victim.

Lesson 68
Take *Every* Opportunity to Broadcast Your Brand

> "By . . . constant renewal of the good report of brave men, the celebrity of those who performed noble deeds is rendered immortal, while at the same time the fame of those who did good service to their country becomes known to the people and a heritage for future generations."
>
> ~Polybius, description of a Roman funeral oration,
> *The Histories*, Book VI

In the year 69 BCE, Julius Caesar's aunt Julia and his wife Cornelia both died suddenly. As a rising young patrician, Caesar made the most of these two painful events by staging elaborate public funerals. Such ceremonies were not in themselves unusual for members of an aristocratic family—especially in the case of the aged and much-venerated Julia. But to do the same for the still young Cornelia, including composing and delivering an oration suitable to a genuine hero of Rome, was unheard of. Caesar did it so well, however, that Romans of all classes and political beliefs applauded it and buzzed approvingly of it. At the very least, they found it the sincere emotional effusion of a kind man and a loving husband.

But it was more—as Caesar knew it would be.

As the historian Polybius explained, the purpose of a Roman funeral oration was to demonstrate and celebrate the role of the deceased in the history and heritage of Rome. To the degree that Julius Caesar succeeded in doing this for his aunt and for his first wife, he also demonstrated and celebrated his own place of destiny in the life of the state and in the hearts of the people. He used the funeral orations, necessitated by a pair of sorrowful personal events, as major public opportunities to establish and broadcast his brand as a well-connected Roman, who possessed a birthright to rule. According to his early biographer Suetonius, Caesar told his listeners: "The family of my aunt Julia is descended from kings on her mother's side and, through her father, from the gods themselves.

For the Marcii Reges, her mother's family, are heirs of Ancus Marcius, fourth king of Rome, while the Julians, of which our clan is a member, descend from the goddess Venus herself. My family therefore holds the sanctity of kings who rule among men and of gods who rule over kings."

By invoking his ancestry through his aunt, Caesar identified himself with a family "brand" long associated with positions of esteem and power. When it came to speaking about his young wife Cornelia to make similar points, he may have both overstepped the bounds of convention and stretched credibility, but he was not a man to pass up such a public opportunity for self-promotion. Even if the people detected some hyperbole in his second funeral oration of the year, they liked what they heard, finding Caesar sincere and worthy.

> **Identify and exploit every** opportunity to create, develop, and broadcast a compelling brand for yourself and your enterprise. Look beyond the obvious. If you cannot effectively follow convention, create, as Caesar did in publicly honoring his dead—young—wife, new conventions effective for you.

■

Lesson 69
Remove Failure as an Option

> "Caesar first had his own horse and then those of all others sent out of sight, thus to equalize the danger of all and to take away the hope of flight."
>
> ~Julius Caesar, *The Gallic War*, Book I

In preparation for the make-or-break Battle of Bibracte, against the Helvetii in Gaul in June of 58 BCE, Caesar deployed his men with great skill, taking care to occupy the high ground. Beyond this tactic, he took another bold step, purposely hiding his horse and the horses of everyone else so that the animals would not loom in the course of battle as a means of retreat and escape. Psychologically, he put the backs of his men to the wall. He did not declare withdrawal to be unacceptable, he gave it the appearance of utter impossibility. In effect, he removed failure as an option.

Nor did Caesar merely impose the ultimatum of do or die upon his legions. Before he hid anyone else's horse, he ordered his own out of sight, determined to "equalize the danger of all," including himself. He did not put his army in harm's way. He led them there. Each, above all he himself, would have to fight his way out, and that meant achieving nothing less than total victory.

The higher the stakes, the greater the motivation. Caesar understood that no stakes were higher than one's own survival. War, he believed, was best fought on the simplest of terms, and so, in preparation for the Battle of Bibracte, he took action to reduce the terms to their most basic. Facing the enemy without means of escape meant victory or death. There was no third alternative. And lest his legions resent the danger in which they were placed, Caesar ensured that he was seen sharing the danger with them. If the stakes were to be high, they were to be equally high for the loftiest commander and the lowliest infantryman.

If you would win, raise the stakes and limit the options that fall short of total triumph. Then be sure that you have skin in the game and that everyone knows it.

■

Lesson 70
Use Competitive Motivation

> "Even if no one else follows, I shall march with the Tenth Legion
> alone; I have no doubt of its allegiance."
>
> ~Julius Caesar, *The Gallic War*, Book I

With his army infected by the sudden fear that Ariovistus and his
Suebi tribal warriors were invincible, Caesar sought to counter
panic with reason (Lesson 39, "Argue Against Panic"). Having
opposed fact against irrational fear, he went on to make a second
appeal based on a competition for glory.

Everyone in his army knew that the Tenth Roman Legion was
Caesar's favorite—and with good reason. It had been raised in Spain
in 61 BCE, when Caesar was governor of Hispania Ulterior (in
English, Further Spain). With the Eighth and Ninth Legions, the
Tenth, with brutal valor, took for Rome what remained unconquered
on the Iberian Peninsula. Among the three legions with Caesar in
Spain, the Tenth proved the most valorous and effective. Now he
held it up as an example, and its effect was transformative: "the
spirit of all ranks was changed in a remarkable fashion." Caesar
wrote that "the greatest keenness and eagerness for active service
was engendered," first among the Tenth Legion itself then among
the other units, who sent senior centurions to Caesar to "give
satisfactory explanation . . . that they had [all along] felt neither
doubt nor panic, and had regarded it as the commander's business,
not their own, to decide the plan of campaign."

The "explanation" was, of course, patently false. The panic had
been real, and the centurions had very definitely questioned
Caesar's command decisions. Having obtained the "remarkable"
transformation he sought, however, Caesar chose to ignore the past
doubts and even the past insubordination. Instead, he
wholeheartedly embraced the renewed spirit of his army. Willfully
choosing to recognize this attitude and orientation as the *only* reality,
he led all his legions into triumphant battle.

Confronted with a crisis of command, Caesar exploited internal competition among his legions by holding up one, the Tenth, above all others, thereby issuing a stern challenge to the rest. Today's prevailing management model tends to emphasize collaboration rather than competition among individuals and departments in an organization. In the long term, collaboration is probably the more effective approach, but in special circumstances or when extraordinary motivation is required, consider playing upon the raw competitive impulse within your enterprise. Caesar's approach bordered on shaming his army. You need not veer toward this negative extreme. Positive modes of competition, including congratulatory email messages and memos, prizes, and award ceremonies, are both friendlier and more constructively celebratory. In some cases, when a special problem must be solved, consider putting "rival" teams or individuals on the job, challenging each to be the first to reach a viable solution.

■

Lesson 71
Be There: Everywhere

"Caesar gave the necessary commands, and then ran down in a chance direction to harangue the troops . . . . He started off at once in the other direction to give a like harangue. . . . The time was so short, the temper of the enemy so ready for conflict."

~Julius Caesar, *The Gallic War*, Book II

As the Battle of the Sabis River (in what is today the French-speaking Walloon region of Belgium) continued to explode, the Nervii led other Belgic troops down the river's steep embankment and into the stream, which was no more than a yard deep. Up from the water they roared, colliding with the Romans on the opposite bank. It was an extraordinary charge, which, Caesar clearly saw, intimidated many of his troops. Accordingly, after issuing "the necessary commands," Caesar, not stopping to ponder the situation, simply "ran down in a chance direction to harangue the troops."

His sole object was to *be there*–to be present in person, among his soldiers, in the heart and heat of combat at its most desperate. What he said to them came from the same artesian well of passion and fire, yet it was not some hollow cheer or, much less, a threat. Instead, speaking from his heart, Caesar issued "no more than a charge [that his troops] . . . bear in mind their ancient valour, to be free from alarm, and bravely to withstand the onslaught of the enemy."

This speech delivered, Caesar ordered his men to engage the enemy, then "started off at once in the other direction to give like harangue" to another of his contingents. He found this group already in the thick of the fight, the time having been "so short, the temper of the enemy so ready for conflict, that there was no space [of time] not only to fit badges in their places, but even to put on helmets and draw covers from shields." It was as if every soldier had caught Caesar's own spirit of immediate action. "In whichever direction each man chanced to come in from the entrenching, whatever standard [banner] each first caught sight of, by that he stood, to lose no fighting time in seeking out his proper company."

By throwing everything into fighting whatever enemy happened to be in front of them, the troops staved off defeat, but at the cost of the disciplined combat formations for which the Roman legions were legendary. This meant that the Belgae were able to isolate the separate Roman units from one another. Fortunately, even so isolated, they fought with such valor that they bought sufficient time for the arrival of reinforcements in the form of the two legions that had been assigned to guard the baggage train.

Encouraged and directed by Caesar, who, with his top lieutenants, continually waded into the melee, appearing, it seemed, everywhere at once, the Romans not only held out but began to restore themselves to more effective fighting formations. For their part, the Nervii and their comrades valiantly and fiercely refused to withdraw, but neither could they penetrate the increasingly dense Roman ranks. Instead, they bloodied themselves against them, as if they were attacking, bodily and over and over again, an unyielding wall.

In the meantime, Caesar was able to bring to bear the kinds of weapons that gave the Romans a great advantage against less technologically developed enemies. The ballista (a kind of giant bow that launched spear-pointed missiles against the enemy), the peltasts (soldiers skilled in hurling javelins), and archers took a heavy toll on Nervii warriors armed only with such short-reach weapons as swords and lances. The Belgic dead were piled so high that fighters on both sides used the accumulating corpses as both ramparts and high ground. The battle ended not with the surrender of the Nervii but with their almost total annihilation.

In the thick of crisis, a leader's place is everywhere. There may be no time for plans, for contemplation, or for strategic maneuver. Time must, however, be made for inspiration, encouragement, and whatever else you can provide to keep the enterprise from dissolving around you. When you find that you are the last available source of order, courage, and hope, make sure you are seen and heard *everywhere*. Show yourself, present yourself, and pass yourself around.

■

Lesson 72
Send a Strong Message

> "He decided that their punishment must be the more severe in order that the privilege of deputies might be more carefully preserved by natives for the future. He therefore put the whole of their senate to the sword, and sold the rest of the men as slaves."
>
> ~Julius Caesar, *The Gallic War*, Book III

Caesar's defeat of the mighty Veneti fleet was total (Lesson 54, "Always Play to Your Advantage"). As the military historian Theodore Ayrault Dodge wrote in 1892, "All the valor, youth and strength of the Veneti had been assembled in this one fleet." With its destruction, this warrior tribe of Brittany had no means of defense and (as Caesar wrote) "Accordingly . . . surrendered themselves and all they had to Caesar." Almost certainly they had heard of Caesar's past acts of mercy to those who surrendered thus abjectly. Perhaps their hope was to claim some of this same mercy. This time, however, the victor resolved to show no mercy whatsoever. Resolving to treat the defeated tribe with utmost severity, he killed the leaders and representatives of the Veneti government, and he sold the flower of the once-powerful tribe's military manhood into abject slavery.

In the centuries that followed this action, generations of statesmen and historians have universally condemned it. No less an ambitious and ruthless conqueror than Napoleon I accused Julius Caesar of gratuitous cruelty. For his own part, Caesar found no difficulty justifying his harsh decision on the grounds that the Veneti had treacherously violated the sacrosanct right of ambassadors in seizing and holding the Roman emissaries prisoner. He was determined to send echoing throughout all Gaul a stark, memorable, and exemplary message, one that would long motivate "natives" to respect "the privilege of deputies" in the future.

From the modern perspective of a world at least ostensibly governed by international treaties and international law, it is impossible to excuse Caesar's cruelty toward the defeated Veneti. From this perspective, however, it is also pointless even to criticize him. Caesar's world was one in which the trade of conqueror was not only accepted but honored and glorified. Conquest, it was universally held, made its own laws.

Tyranny, vengeance, and cruelty are neither desirable nor viable constituents of leadership in modern enterprise. Nevertheless, Caesar's motive in exercising these very elements was (he himself explained) to send an enduring message, and that is something all leaders in every age and circumstance must possess the capacity to deliver. Your directives need not be harsh and should never be threatening. They must, however, be clear, strong, unapologetic, and, above all, unambiguously compelling.

Lesson 73
To Be Proactive Be Predictive

> "Although Caesar had not yet learnt their designs, yet the misfortune of his ships and the fact that the chiefs had broken off the surrender of hostages led him to suspect that events would turn out as they did; and therefore he prepared means to meet any emergency."
>
> ~Julius Caesar, *The Gallic War*, Book IV

Caesar got himself into trouble in Britain, having landed with too few men and little baggage in a place about which he knew very little indeed. Among the many things he did not know was the "day of the month which usually makes the highest tides in the Ocean."

This deficiency of knowledge resulted in the sinking of many of his transports, a catastrophe that "caused great dismay throughout the army. For there were no other ships to carry them back." Worse, "everything needful for the repair of ships was lacking; and as it was generally understood that the army was to winter in Gaul, no corn [cereal crops] had been provided in these parts against the winter." Even worse for Caesar, his own army was not the only group that became aware of these dire straits. The British chieftains, who had been negotiating their surrender and general peace terms with the Roman invaders, now conspired anew against the Romans, and, "departing a few at a time from the [Roman] camp, they began secretly to draw in their followers from the fields."

Because their withdrawal from the camp was subtle and their conspiracy carried out in secrecy, Caesar did not learn directly of their intentions. Nevertheless, he accurately read the signs, noting especially that the chiefs had suddenly "broken off the surrender of hostages." Accordingly, he took proactive steps "to meet any emergency," including collecting wheat and other cereal crops daily from the fields and stockpiling them in camp, and then salvaging the "timber and bronze of the ships which had been most severely damaged to repair the rest." Given clearly necessary, positive work to do, the troops were invigorated, their morale lifted, and they set about their tasks "most zealously."

> **Adopt a posture that** is both predictive and proactive. Read the signs, then act in accordance with them—and do so sooner rather than later. Prediction without action generally creates anxiety and erodes morale; therefore, put your organization into action before the situation proves itself critical.

■

Lesson 74
Go Back to Italy

> "... to go to Italy, as it was his practice every year to do ..."
> ~Julius Caesar, *The Gallic War*, Book V

Some, perhaps most, historians refer to Julius Caesar's seven-year conquest of Gaul as the "Gallic Wars," but in his own history, Caesar called the campaigns of 58 to 51 BCE the *Bello Gallico:* the "Gallic War." The implication is that he regarded these campaigns as phases of a single great project he was determined to complete from beginning to end. In the process, of course, he not only acquired a vast empire for Rome, he built his own matchless reputation, which allowed him to become the most powerful man in the Roman world.

To put it as a gross understatement, the Gallic War was time and effort well invested. Nevertheless, as Caesar himself also realized, it was time spent very far from the centers of political power in Italy and Rome. Believing it fatal to lose contact with these centers, Caesar made it his custom to employ the winter of each campaign year (for armies in the ancient world generally shunned combat in wintertime) to return closer to the heart of the Republic.

You cannot afford to lose touch with the centers of control and sources of power. Manage your schedule to balance time in the field with time for necessary politics and diplomacy. You must achieve great things, but you also must be seen and heard, even as you see and hear others.

■

Lesson 75
Avoid Relying on the Moment

> "[Titurius] ran hither and thither posting cohorts, yet even this he did in timid fashion and with all judgment evidently gone, as generally happens when men are forced to decide in the moment of action."
>
> ~Julius Caesar, *The Gallic War*, Book V

In the winter of 45 BCE, legions under two of Caesar's most trusted legates (generals), Lucius Aurunculeius Cotta and Quintus Titurius Sabinus, were attacked by Belgic insurgents at Atuatuca Tungrorum, modern Tongeren (Tongres) in what is today the Limburg province of Belgium. The commanders were very much at odds with one another as to how to respond to the attack. Cotta proposed holding fast against the onslaught, whereas Titurius wanted to yield the Roman position and withdraw under the protection of Ambiorix, prince of the Eburones tribe (of northern Gaul), which was ostensibly allied with Rome. Cotta, however, did not trust Ambiorix—and, as it turned out, with good reason. He soon proved treacherous, leading the Romans into a double ambush.

In the meantime, Titurius responded to the attack with panic and ineffectual action, his "judgment evidently gone" (according to Caesar), whereas Cotta, having long suspected treachery from Ambiorix, was better prepared for any attack. Caesar writes that Cotta "neglected nothing for the safety of the force," although he does not specify just what provisions Cotta made, other than delivering a very effective exhortation and encouragement to his troops. Nevertheless, in his *Gallic War*, Caesar draws a sharp contrast between Titurius's dithering panic and Cotta's well-prepared systematic response—though, in the end, neither prevailed against the Gallic onslaught.

We tend to place a high value on the ability to "think on your feet." Caesar, who was notable for precisely this quality as well as for his remarkably cool courage even in the heat of apparently hopeless battle, clearly distrusted spontaneity. He believed that being forced to make a critical decision "in the moment of action" typically resulted in a bad decision. As a commander, Caesar personally took every possible step to avoid relying on his ability to make a snap decision. Instead, he believed in gathering intelligence and making adequate plans and preparations that assured an uninterrupted line of supply and a battlefield of his own choosing. Spontaneity is a valuable tool for survival, but operating safely, comfortably, and efficiently according to a well-designed plan is a more certain route to success rather than mere survival. Do whatever you can to avoid having to rely on improvisation and the inspiration of a moment.

■

Lesson 76
Don't Be Damned by a Damn Good Defense

> "It diminished the hope of our own troops and made the enemy keener for the fight, since the movement could not but betray the greatest apprehension and despair."
>
> ~Julius Caesar, *Gallic War*, Book V

Under severe attack, the gallant Roman commander Lucius Aurunculeius Cotta (see Lesson 75, "Avoid Relying on the Moment") ordered his troops to abandon their baggage and "form square"—that is, deploy in the defensive "infantry square" formation for which the Roman legions were famous.

Caesar wrote that this defensive plan was "not reprehensible in such an emergency." The square, in which troops arranged themselves in at least three lines around a reserve in the center, provided a 360-degree defensive perimeter that was a kind of portable fortress—stable, yet also capable of rapid movement. It was a time-tested tactic. Caesar pointed out, however, that, in this instance, it "had an unfortunate result; for it diminished the hope of our own troops and made the enemy keener for the fight, since the movement could not but betray the greatest apprehension and despair."

While "forming square" had been the tactically sound decision of a brave man, Cotta, it nevertheless failed because it eroded morale. Instead of protecting them, as Cotta believed it would, the order to form square gave the soldiers a reason to be fearful. Yet worse, even as that order sent a message of fear to the Romans, it also broadcast the same message to the Belgic attackers, giving them reason to believe that the Romans had been beaten and were ripe for finishing off. This impression was made the stronger by a breakdown in vaunted Roman discipline, as soldiers deserted "their standards"—their cohort banners—and each soldier "hastened to seek and to seize from the baggage-train all that he accounted dearest."

With morale shattered, the legions ceased to be an army, so that "everything was a confusion of shouting and weeping." In the end, both commanders were killed: Cotta, heroically in the thick of battle, "hit full in the face by a sling-bullet," and Titurius, ignominiously surrounded and slain by the warriors into whose camp Ambiorix, under a false flag of truce, had led him.

During all of this, Caesar was in his winter quarters in Italy. Learning of the insurgency against Roman authority in Gaul, he hastened back to Gaul to rescue his forces.

Julius Caesar knew Lucius Aurunculeius Cotta to be a brave commander and a competent one. Under his co-commander, Quintus Titurius Sabinus, the Romans panicked when attacked. Cotta, however, was able to impose discipline by forming them into the defensive square they had so often drilled and rehearsed. Brave and competent, Cotta was not, however, a great commander. "Forming square" was strictly by-the-book leadership, when what was required in the desperate situation he and his men faced was truly inspired and inspiring leadership. Caesar understood that the problem inherent in going on the defensive was the danger of a collapse of morale, a loss of hope, and the onset of panic that creates a chaos in which soldiers cease to function as an army and become instead a frightened crowd.

The great nineteenth- and early-twentieth-century psychologist and philosopher William James wrote, "We do not run because we are frightened, we are frightened because we run." Putting an enterprise on an obviously defensive footing may be intended as the product of prudence, but it can result in actually producing fear. The greatest—and most successful— generals have always believed that safety is achieved through victory, that an army in forward motion is safer than an army hunkered down, and that an army charging headlong toward the enemy is safest of all.

■

Lesson 77
Replace Blame with Praise

> "The next day he [Caesar] held a parade [military review] and set
> forth all that had occurred, cheering and encouraging the troops,
> and admonishing them to bear with the greater equanimity the
> loss incurred [earlier] through the fault and foolhardiness of a
> general [Lucius Aurunculeius Cotta and/or Quintus Titurius
> Sabinus], inasmuch as by the goodness of the immortal gods and
> by their own valour the misfortune had been made good, leaving
> to the enemy no lasting joy, to themselves no long-enduring grief."
>
> ~Julius Caesar, *The Gallic War*, Book V

Caesar believed his timely return to Gaul and victory over the
treacherous Gallic-Celtic leader Ambiorix "made good" the
disastrous defeat of Lucius Aurunculeius Cotta and Quintus
Titurius Sabinus at the hands of Belgic insurgents (see Lesson 75,
"Avoid Relying on the Moment," and Lesson 76, "Don't Be Damned
by a Damn Good Defense"). Unwilling to assume that his troops,
left to themselves, would arrive at this same interpretation of events,
Caesar took active steps to ensure that they shared his view of the
situation: that their most recent triumph was more than sufficient to
erase the earlier humiliation of Roman arms.

To put his crucial message across, Caesar held a "parade,"
which, in military terminology, is a combination ceremony, troop
review, and drill, a simultaneous celebration and application as well
as demonstration of discipline. On this occasion, Caesar did not
merely review his troops, as commanders customarily do when they
order a parade, but he enthusiastically cheered and encouraged
them. He boldly and blatantly "spun" the sequence of events—the
humiliating Roman defeat under Cotta and Titurius followed by
the victory he himself led. His point was not to picture the slain
Cotta and Titurius as inferior generals to himself, but to transfer all
blame for the defeat from the soldiers before him and place it
entirely in the "fault and foolhardiness of a general" while he

generously attributed his own subsequent victory to the soldiers' "valour." In this way, Caesar purged blame and replaced it with praise. Moreover, he also gave a role to the "goodness of the immortal gods," thereby implying that Roman defeat had been a temporary aberration, the merest stumble en route to victory, which was the glorious outcome sanctioned by the gods and by destiny, forces, Caesar strongly implied, that were on the side of Rome and the soldiers of Rome.

> **When an error is** corrected and a problem solved, quickly shift the focus from the negative—the error and the problem—to the positive: the correction and the solution. In doing so, wholly replace blame for the mistake or the difficulty with praise for the repair and the resolution. To motivate your enterprise, celebrate its success rather than mourn its failure.

■

Lesson 78
A Leader Leads

> "As far as I am concerned I would rather be the first man here
> than the second in Rome."
>
> ~Julius Caesar quoted in Plutarch, *Life of Caesar*

In the year 61 BCE, Caesar was named governor of Hispania Ulterior (Further Spain). The biographer-historian Plutarch wrote that, as Caesar crossed the Alps on his way to assume his new post, he passed through a tiny, desolate, hopelessly backward village, ". . . altogether a miserable-looking place." His friends were laughing and joking about it, saying: 'No doubt here too one would find people pushing themselves forward to gain office, and here too there are struggles to get the first place and jealous rivalries among the great men.'"

Caesar turned to them: "As far as I am concerned I would rather be the first man here than the second in Rome." He was not laughing.

> **A leader does not** whine about the organization she leads. She does not complain about what her enterprise lacks. She does not idly speculate on how much better off she would be if this or that were larger, richer, better, or simply different. She does not excuse herself or her company. A leader leads.

■

Lesson 79
Appeal to Self-Interest

> "Caesar lavished generous rewards, which showed that he was not piling up wealth from his wars for his private luxury or a life of ease; rather he laid it aside in trust as a prize for bravery which was open to all."
>
> ~Plutarch, *Life of Caesar*

Caesar was a close observer of human nature and human behavior. A dedicated student of motivation, it didn't take him long to arrive at the bottom line. The single most reliable motivator of the actions of human beings, he concluded, was self-interest. Accordingly, the use of direct and desirable rewards was his motivational tool of choice.

As drivers of achievement, rewards offered him considerable leverage. Good and valuable in themselves, rewards also sent a strong message, which the historian Plutarch clearly recognized: Caesar was not selfishly "piling up wealth from his wars for his private luxury," exploiting the lives and labor of others to satisfy himself, but was eager to share the bounty among everyone who played a part in having acquired it. Thus to self-interest, Caesar added the motive of an implied appeal to a universal sense of justice. Not only did he demonstrate his own freedom from selfish motives, he also judged—and thereby rewarded—his soldiers (according to the historian Suetonius) "by their fighting record, not by their . . . social position."

You may make use of a wide variety of motivational tools. At bottom, the overwhelming majority of these are variations on the theme of self-interest. The simplest and surest way to get people to do what you want them to do is to persuade them that it is in their self-interest to do so. Reward performance generously, justly, and consistently.

■

Lesson 80
Give the Word

"*Quirites.*"

~Julius Caesar, quoted in Nic Fields, *Julius Caesar: Leadership, Strategy, Conflict*

Trained as a lawyer and orator, Caesar, who also possessed prodigious natural gifts as a historical writer, was exquisitely mindful of the language he used. As the military historian Nic Fields points out, he created a special bond with his troops, especially those of his favorite Tenth Legion, in part through the choice of the title by which he addressed them. Whereas the standard military form of address for soldiers was *milites*—simply, "soldiers"—Caesar preferred *commilitones*, "comrades" or, even more accurately, "brothers in arms."

By upping the emotional ante in his relationship with his men by elevating them from subordinates to collaborators, Caesar endowed them with a lofty status he could, if need be, also take away. The Tenth Legion was probably raised in Spain during 61–60 BCE and served with Caesar through the Gallic War (58–49 BCE) and the Civil Wars (49–45 BCE). During the latter conflict, sheer exhaustion seems to have propelled the unit to the brink of mutiny. Caesar pulled his men back from that brink not by pleading with them and even less by offering threats, but through the use of a one-word rebuke. He assembled the troops and addressed his disgruntled soldiers not as *commilitones* nor even as *milites*, but as *quirites*.

On the face of it, this was no insult. *Quiris* was the time-honored word for a Roman citizen—a title much coveted in the ancient world. Applied to a soldier on the verge of betraying his commander, however, the word must have hit like a hammer blow. It signified a fall from the status of Caesar's comrade at arms to a mere civilian. And because we know how skilled Caesar was with words, we can be certain that an added sardonic twist did not escape him. *Quiris*, "citizen," was the very same Latin word as "spear." Even in demoting his comrades to civilians, Caesar reminded them of the military identity, duty, and allegiance they now threatened to betray and forsake.

> **Build constructive, productive relationships** with every single word you use. Begin by shedding singular pronouns—*I, you, mine, yours*—wherever and whenever you can. Replace them with plurals: *we, us, our, ours*. Create common cause, collegiality, and comradeship.

■

Lesson 81
Conquer by Kindness

> "Let us try whether . . . we can win back the goodwill of all and enjoy a lasting victory, seeing that others have not managed by cruelty to escape hatred or to make their victories endure, except Lucius Sulla, whom I do not intend to imitate. Let this be the new style of conquest, to make mildness and generosity our shield."
>
> ~Julius Caesar, letter to his agents in Rome, March 5, 49 BCE, quoted in Cicero's *Epistulae ad Atticum*

Julius Caesar came of age politically in the era of Lucius Cornelius Sulla (ca. 138–78 BCE), who served twice as consul and also as dictator of the Roman Republic. As a military commander, he was never defeated, and in many ways he was also a remarkable statesman and ruler. He is remembered most, however, for his ruthlessly bloody policy of executing anyone and everyone he perceived to be an enemy of the state or of himself. In the space of a year, he officially sent some fifteen hundred rival nobles to their deaths, and historians believe that the toll during his dictatorship was probably closer to nine thousand. For all of this bloodshed, Sulla did not leave the Roman Republic more stable than he had found it. Many of his reforms were repealed shortly after his death, and the allegiance of the army remained a critical issue. Instead of answering to the Senate, soldiers owed allegiance to their general—a state of affairs that virtually assured repeated conflict and even civil war.

Both Pompey the Great and Julius Caesar clearly took inspiration from Sulla in rising to power; however, Caesar, who had certainly shown himself capable of "cruelty" in Gaul and other arenas of conflict, was determined not to make the same mistakes as Sulla. Having defeated Pompey and his followers in the Civil War, Caesar sought a policy of reconciliation through a demonstration of "goodwill" in which "mildness and generosity [would be] our shield."

> **From a position of** demonstrated strength dispense justice, generosity, encouragement, and understanding. Fear may coerce compliance, but it will never create anything more than a counterfeit loyalty.

■

Lesson 82
What Have You Done for Me Lately?

"More people worship the rising than the setting sun."
~ Pompey the Great, quoted by Plutarch in *Life of Pompey*

Gnaeus Pompeius Magnus (106–48 BCE)—Pompey the Great—was an extraordinarily successful Roman general. He came of age as a military commander in service to his father, Gnaeus Pompeius Strabo, from whom, at the age of nineteen, he inherited his wealth, his estates, and his political and military influence. In service to the ruthless dictator Lucius Cornelius Sulla, Pompey campaigned in Sicily, securing that island in 82 BCE as a source of grain for Rome and then defeating Sulla's enemies in Africa. There, in Africa, his legions proclaimed him Imperator and, on his return to Rome, Sulla personally bestowed upon him the cognomen of Magnus—making him Pompey the Great. Sulla, however, withheld from Pompey the highest award of a "triumph," a public procession of honor, and ordered him immediately to disband his legions. When Pompey defied him, refusing to dismiss his loyal men, Sulla backed down, and Pompey continued his rise.

After the death of Sulla in 78 BCE, the Senate sent Pompey the Great to Hispania (Spain), where, between 76 and 71 BCE, he first defeated the enemies of the Senate and then turned to combat the remarkably successful army of Spartacus, ending the great slave rebellion in Rome's costly Third Servile War.

Pompey's victories in Spain and his defeat of Spartacus made him a popular hero. He was hailed as the greatest of all Roman generals and in 70 BCE was elevated, along with Marcus Licinius Crassus, to the office of consul. Two years later, Pompey led a successful war against pirates who menaced Roman trade and by the mid 60s was hailed as the "first man" of Rome. He went on to defeat Rome's long-standing enemy, Mithridates VI of Pontus (a kingdom located in modern northeastern Turkey). Then he conquered Syria, established Roman hegemony in Phoenicia, and captured Jerusalem, making Judea a Roman province.

In 61 BCE, Pompey, Crassus, and Caesar entered into a grand, albeit unofficial, alliance, which became the First Triumvirate, with Caesar as consul. At the end of his consulship, Caesar assumed command in Gaul while Pompey served as governor of Hispania Ulterior (southwestern Spain and Portugal). During this period, Caesar conquered Gaul, a feat that elevated him above both Crassus and Pompey in the public eye. In 53 BCE, Crassus and most of his army were killed in combat with the Parthians at Carrhae (in modern Turkey). This pitted Pompey against Caesar for sole control of Rome and set the stage for the Civil War of 49–45 BCE between Caesar and the Optimates, led by Pompey.

The Civil War of 49–45 BCE was very hard fought. Since most of what is known about it, however, derives from Caesar's firsthand history, it is not surprising that Pompey comes across as an inferior general. Objectively viewed, he had compiled a remarkable record of conquest. But he was old by the time of the Civil War, and, even more important, whereas Caesar had spent some eight years continuously at war, mostly in Gaul, greatly expanding Rome's empire, Pompey, at the outbreak of the Civil War, had not seen military action since 62 BCE. Pompey's ultimate defeat in the conflict as well as the general perception that he was not in the same league as Caesar (who was acclaimed as a military genius) is due less to a deficiency in his innate abilities than to the long period of his military idleness. For us today, the takeaway lesson of Pompey's downfall and defeat is starkly simple. He could not satisfactorily answer the "classic" question by which performance is most often evaluated: *What have you done for me lately?*

■

6

The Valor
Proposition

Lesson 83
Aim Higher

> "Mother, today you will see your son as pontifex maximus—
> or as a fugitive."
>
> ~Julius Caesar, quoted in Plutarch, *Life of Caesar*

By the year 63 BCE, Julius Caesar had been a lawyer and for the past ten years a pontifex, one of perhaps a dozen priests who supervised religious ceremonies and affairs in Rome, and since 65 BCE, aedile, one of several officials essentially in charge of maintaining the infrastructure of the city of Rome and managing public spectacles. He enjoyed some degree of prominence, but, at thirty-seven years old, Caesar recognized that he was no longer a youngster and was anxious to leap ahead politically.

As pontifex, he understood that the highest religious office in Rome was that of pontifex maximus, the priest who not only led the priests, but who represented them in the Senate. The office was highly visible, and it even came with an official state residence, the Domus Publica.

On its face, it was hardly unreasonable for a serving pontifex to aspire to pontifex maximus, and when the incumbent, Quintus Metellus Pius, died of old age in 63 BCE, the opening seemed to Caesar an opportunity too good to ignore. The trouble was that there were two far more likely candidates waiting in the wings. Both Quintus Lutatius Catulus and Publius Servilius Isauricus, highly esteemed senators, were older and more distinguished than he, possessed of what today would be called greater "gravitas" than the comparatively lowly aedile. To step forward against such men as candidate for pontifex maximus was, in fact, the height of temerity.

As aedile, Caesar had already borrowed prodigiously in order to fund public events and spectacles sufficiently lavish to impress jaded Romans. He now doubled down, borrowing even more to fund the bribes that were very much a part of Roman politics. Bribing the electors who had the power to raise him to the exalted office he sought was not a crime, provided you didn't get caught. Caesar exercised all his charm and wit to ensure that he did not. Moreover, he avoided simply pouring out money, but instead carefully orchestrated his campaign of bribery, using a coterie of friends, political allies, and paid agents to work on the electors.

It was nevertheless a very long shot, and, according to Caesar's early biographer, Plutarch, Aurelia, his mother, wept on the morning of the election. She believed her son had put himself—and the Julii family—in a terrible fix. If he lost the election, his creditors would ruin them all. In a dark effort to reassure her, as Caesar left the family house that morning to await the results at the Domus Publica, he kissed her cheek and declared, "Mother, today you will see your son as pontifex maximus—or as a fugitive."

The Romans of Caesar's day certainly knew the Greek myth of Icarus, the boy who, wearing the wax wings his father Daedalus had fashioned, flew higher and higher until, too near the sun, the wings melted, and he tumbled out of the sky and to his death. Caesar certainly understood the risks of aiming higher. You could fall farther. Aiming lower, he understood, entailed less risk. Instead, it carried certainty—the certainty of mediocrity. For him, such a certainty was unacceptable. Stepping to the forefront, which is *the* defining act of leadership, always means risk. Live with it, or live a life somewhere in the middle of the enterprise. As for Caesar, he won the election.

Lesson 84
Create Transparency

> "Caesar put the lieutenant-generals and the quartermaster-general each in command of a legion, that every man might have their witness of his valour."
>
> ~Julius Caesar, *The Gallic War*, Book I

In preparing the order of the great showdown battle against the German forces led by Ariovistus, chieftain of the Suebi, Caesar arranged his battle lines so that the commanders he personally placed at the head of each legion were conspicuously visible, enabling "every man" to bear "witness" to their valor. This high visibility—such utter and total transparency—would work two ways. It would provide for all soldiers a model of courage and zeal, and it would ensure that the top commanders, placed thus onstage by the highest commander, would be motivated to consistently lead with the requisite courage and zeal. Like General George S. Patton Jr. some two thousand years later, Julius Caesar wanted all of his men, including the lowliest foot soldier, to see (as Patton put it) "that a general can get shot" just as a private can get shot. By the same token, also like Caesar, Patton wanted his commanders to feel the eyes of their men burning into them, just as he wanted the men to feel themselves under the unblinking scrutiny of their commander.

Caesar knew that soldiers fight courageously for many reasons, ranging from pay to patriotism. But he recognized the existence of one motive to bold action that was more powerful than any other. It was the good opinion of one's comrades and commanders. Caesar had a remarkably modern understanding of the psychology of the common soldier. In any effective army, the bonds among troops are strong. While some men may sacrifice for love of country, far more do so out of love for one another—what may be called *esprit de* *corps* or "comradeship." Just as soldiers fight their hardest out of high regard for one another, so the members of any enterprise with a lofty level of morale strive for the common good—to satisfy and advance themselves as well as the other members of the team. For Caesar, the function of transparency was to motivate valorous conduct. He believed this to be a more immediate and therefore powerful inducement than any abstract appeal to the glory of Rome.

Do you want to improve performance? Put it on display always and everywhere.

■

Lesson 85
Demand and Enable Self-Reliance

> "The stress of the moment was relieved by . . . the knowledge and experience of the troops—for their training in previous battles enabled them to appoint for themselves what was proper to be done as readily as others could have shown them."
>
> ~Julius Caesar, *The Gallic War*, Book II

The Nervii were the most remotely located of the Belgae and, in Caesar's estimation, the most ruthless, dangerous, and inherently warlike of the tribes. He compared their way of life to that of the ancient Spartans, legendary to the Romans as they are to our modern selves. The Belgae were a hard people, lean and abstemious. They shunned all luxuries and had no truck with traders or merchants (at least according to Caesar; archaeological evidence suggests a culture somewhat more indulgent, open, and less severe). While Caesar's initial success against certain of the Belgic tribes prompted some surrenders among tribal commanders, the Roman victories served only to motivate the Nervii to unite with Atrebates and Viromandui in an attack against Caesar's legions at the Battle of the Sabis, fought in 57 BCE along the Selle River near the modern northern French town of Saulzoir close to the Belgian border.

Caesar led a total of eight legions deep into the land of the Belgae, six veteran legions in front and two freshly recruited legions guarding the baggage train in the rear. He halted at the Sabis River and began setting up his infantry encampment while his cavalry and auxiliary forces lashed out at tribal refugees and fugitives at large in the vicinity of the camp. This brought the cavalry into contact with outlying Nervii forces, whose presence tipped Caesar off to the proximity of the main Nervii army under Boduognatus, a warlord of considerable renown. Rather than wait for Boduognatus to cross the Sabis and attack him, Caesar followed his customary combat pattern, which was to seize the initiative and lead a preemptive attack. So eager was he to get the drop on the enemy, that many of his troops were still busy constructing the camp when Caesar suddenly ordered the attack. Perceiving that the Roman offensive was less than full strength, Boduognatus launched from out of the dense woods a fierce counterattack, which overwhelmed Caesar before he could fully consolidate his forces.

The Roman cavalry, Caesar readily admitted, was "easily beaten and thrown into disorder, and with incredible speed the enemy rushed down to the river, so that almost at the same moment they were seen at the edge of the woods, in the river, and then at close quarters. Then with the same speed [they had used in the attack against the Roman cavalry] they hastened up-hill against our camp and the troops engaged in entrenching it."

It was a tidal wave—the kind of lethal assault that engulfs armies by its very simultaneity along a wide front. As Caesar himself put it, he "had everything to do at one moment—the flag to raise, as signal of a general call to arms; the trumpet-call to sound; the troops to recall from entrenching; the men to bring in who had gone somewhat farther afield in search of stuff for the [siege] ramp; the line to form; the troops to harangue; the signal to give." It seemed hopeless, for a "great part of these duties was prevented by the shortness of the time and the advance of the enemy."

In writing about the battle, Caesar did not hesitate to confess that immediate defeat was averted not through his own martial prowess—indeed, he had committed the potentially catastrophic error of prematurely ordering an attack—but because of "the knowledge and experience of the troops" themselves. *They* knew what to do, and they did it on their own initiative, without a commander issuing orders. True, Caesar further pointed out that he forbade "the several lieutenant-generals to leave the entrenching and their proper legions until the camp was fortified," in this way preventing the camp itself from being completely overrun, but the main credit for salvation had to be awarded to the soldiers: their self-reliance and capacity for independent action. The successful defense of the Roman camp was an example of what military historians call a "soldiers' battle," a fighting exchange in which victory is achieved or defeat averted not through the planning and presence of top brass, but by sheer dint of valor, skill, and effort on the part of every soldier.

Some two thousand years after Caesar, General George S. Patton, Jr., the great American commander of World War II, jotted in his field notebook this sentence: "The soldier is the army."

It could just as well have been written by the Roman himself—or, indeed, by most any of history's "great captains." A leader is powerless without an able and willing organization to execute his plans and orders. It is the organization that gives shape, substance, and action to the executive's intentions, and that organization consists of individuals, who must follow orders but who must also possess the capacity, the training, the motivation, and the permission to carry out their assignments creatively and effectively, especially in the face of unanticipated crisis. If an enterprise is to be more than a mere mechanism, critically vulnerable to breakdown, its members must be given the tools, the means, and the mission of self-reliance.

Caesar gave his men credit for his army's salvation at the Sabis River, but it was he, their commander, who had seen to their training, their motivation, and their understanding of their mission. It was he who enabled the deliverance they most assuredly accomplished.

■

Lesson 86
"Place All Hope of Safety in Courage"

"The only hope . . . was to try the last expedient of making a sortie."

~Julius Caesar, *The Gallic War*, Book III

Despite his success in Gaul, Caesar knew it was dangerous to stay far away and remote from the political intrigues and intricacies of Rome. He therefore returned to Italy for the winter of 57–56 BCE, sending Servius Sulpicius Galba as legate (commanding general) of the Twelfth Legion, together with some supporting cavalry, to deal with Gallic tribes causing trouble south of what is today the Lake of Geneva. The Nantuates, Veragri, and Seduni tribes (all of which occupied parts of modern Switzerland) were routinely and violently interfering with the passage of merchants and settlers across the Alps and into the Rhône valley.

Galba quickly defeated the troublemakers, then camped in the Rhône valley along one bank of the Rhône River. Bristling at their own recent defeat, resentful that Galba had taken many of their children as hostages, and fearing imminent annexation to Rome, a coalition of Gallic tribes decided to attack Galba's solitary legion.

After stealthily occupying the heights and passes surrounding Galba's camp, cutting off the Twelfth Legion from both sustenance and reinforcement, they prepared to attack.

When Galba recognized the full extent of his dire situation, he convened a council of war. Although outnumbered, he and his commanders decided that their best hope was to hold the camp and withstand the coming attack as best they could. When that attack came, however, it was far more severe than they had imagined. Recounting the assault presumably from Galba's own report, Caesar wrote that "the enemy, upon a signal given, charged down from all sides, and hurled volleys of stones and javelins against the [hastily erected Roman] rampart." The men of the Twelfth Legion resisted for six exhausting hours, consuming in this period all of their own javelins and other thrown ammunition. With their ammunition exhausted, Galba recognized that the only hope left to them was to cut their way out of the siege with their swords. He accordingly ordered his troops to collect as many "of the missiles discharged against them" as possible. After briefly refreshing themselves, they were, "upon a given signal" to take up their salvaged weapons and use them to aid in making a breakthrough—to "burst from the camp," placing "all hope of safety in courage."

Courage, in the end, proved to be the most potent weapon of all.

"They did as they were bid," Caesar wrote, "and suddenly from all the gates a sortie was made, leaving the enemy no chance of learning what was afoot, nor of rallying. So there was a complete change of fortune; the Romans surrounded on every side and slew the multitude which had come in hope of capturing the camp, and of more than thirty thousand [Gallic] men . . . more than a third were slain, while the rest were driven in headlong flight."

Common sense and an instinct for survival dictate that the possession of an exit strategy is far preferable to facing annihilation with no way out. Yet sometimes you do find yourself with no exit. In such a case, you have a choice to make: whether to yield to "reality" and give up, or seek to transform reality by harnessing the one commodity you have left—courage. It is hardly comfortable to fight with your back to the wall, yet that most anxious and painful position offers one distinct advantage: an unyielding launch pad for a counterattack in a single uncompromising and unremitting direction—forward, against the enemy, against the problem, against the threat.

True, a wall against your back is a hard, unforgiving opportunity. Use it, and you may effect a "complete change of fortune"—or you may fail. Choose not to use it, however, and failure is the only possible outcome.

■

Lesson 87
Manage Fear, Deploy Intimidation

"Frightened . . . our troops did not press on with the same fire and force as they were accustomed to show in land engagements."
~Julius Caesar, *The Gallic War*, Book IV

Caesar had taken care to find the safest site possible when he landed on Britain for the first time (see Lesson 58, "Choose a Safe Landing"), but disembarkation nevertheless proved "a matter of extreme difficulty." For one thing, Caesar's large transports "could not be run ashore, except in deep water," and "the troops—though they did not know the ground, had not their hands free, and were loaded with the great and grievous weight of their arms—had nevertheless at one and the same time to leap down from the vessels, to stand firm in the waves, and to fight the enemy." That enemy, in contrast to them, was unencumbered: "had all their limbs free, and knew the ground exceeding well." The enemy stood either on dry land or waded a little into the water and "boldly hurled their missiles, or spurred on their horses, which were trained to it." With all the advantages apparently on the side of the enemy, the Romans were understandably frightened and intimidated.

Seeing that the chief problem was one of fear, Caesar decided to manage that emotion by finding a means to turn the fear *against* the Britons. But how? They had the advantage of fighting–with both hands, no less–from dry land and on land with which they were intimately familiar.

Such were the enemy's advantages. Turning from these, Caesar quickly inventoried his own assets. He decided that the most formidable advantage he possessed were his mighty ships, especially the combat ships, as opposed to his transports. These, he believed, were extraordinarily intimidating instruments of war, especially to members of a primitive island tribe. He therefore "commanded the ships of war (which [in contrast to the transport vessels] were less familiar in appearance to the natives, and could move more freely at need) to remove a little from the transports, to row at speed, and to bring up on the exposed flank of the enemy." Caesar saw that his men were afraid of the unknown as embodied in the island of Britain. To the Britons, however, the Roman warships represented the unknown and were therefore a means of inducing fear in them.

As Caesar had hoped and predicted, the sight of the highly maneuverable warships, so much less familiar to the natives than the transport vessels, was greatly intimidating. To this psychological effect, he added firepower, clearing the Britons off "with slings, arrows, and artillery."

Caesar reported, "This movement proved of great service to our troops; for the natives, frightened by the shape of the ships, the motion of the oars, and the unfamiliar type of the artillery, came to a halt, and retired"–albeit "only for a little space." The situation was thus improved, but not resolved. Moreover, the Romans still "hung back, chiefly on account of the depth of the sea." Fortunately for

Caesar, the eagle-bearer of the Tenth Legion—the lead soldier, whose responsibility it was to bear the Roman eagle standard into battle— took the initiative and managed fear in yet a different way.

"Leap down," he called out to his fellow soldiers, "unless you wish to betray your eagle to the enemy; it shall be told that I at any rate did my duty to my country and my general."

The enemy having withdrawn, even slightly, the eagle-bearer's example and the specter of the shame of cowardice were enough to overcome the inertia of fear. As the eagle-bearer "cast himself forth from the ship" and advanced with his standard against the enemy, the troops began to exhort "one another not to allow so dire a disgrace." They "leapt down from the ship with one accord." When the troops on the other ships saw them, "they likewise followed on, and drew near to the enemy."

Fear is a powerful driver of action. Properly managed, it can drive productive action. Left unmanaged, it can destroy an operation and even bring down the organization itself. Do not deny or shun fear. Understand it. Use it as you would any other motivating energy.

■

Lesson 88
Suck It Up

"[Caesar] never allowed his weakened health to slow him down, but instead used the life of a soldier as therapy. He marched endlessly, ate simple food, slept outside, and endured every hardship. In this way, he strengthened his body against illness."

~Plutarch, *Life of Caesar*

Julius Caesar was a man of impressive physical stature for his time, nearly six feet tall, and appeared to be in excellent physical condition. Lean and muscular, he had the physique of a soldier, which stood in stark contrast to some of the more pampered and even decadent patrician politicians surrounding him.

Much like President John F. Kennedy, whose youthful vigor and good looks disguised the array of debilitating ailments from which he suffered, Caesar's fit appearance belied chronically ill health. Migraine headaches prostrated him from time to time, but most familiar to historians was his epilepsy, which the ancients called the "falling sickness." It seemed to afflict Caesar most when he endured the physical hardships of military campaigning, and his fits apparently presented all the dramatic and frightening features of the classic grand mal seizure. Despite this affliction, Caesar pushed himself as hard as he pushed his soldiers, who marched faster and farther than any other army, heedless of weather, hunger, and topography alike.

Plutarch believed that the hardships of a soldier's life actually gave Caesar strength. Perhaps they did, perhaps they did not. But whether harsh conditions helped or hurt him, Caesar was determined to endure them.

Leaders are human beings, and challenges come to human beings in all forms—intellectual, emotional, and physical. As to the physical challenges, at times there is only one reliably and finally effective approach. Suck it up. Persevere. Endure.

Lesson 89
Invest in a Scarlet Cloak

> "The conspicuous colour of the cloak he habitually wore in battle proclaimed his arrival."
>
> ~Julius Caesar, *The Gallic War*, Book VII

Caesar fought the Battle of Alesia, near modern Alise-Sainte-Reine, France, in the fall of 52 BCE with the objective of capturing the hill fort of the local Mandubii tribe, part of the grand Gallic confederation led by the formidable Arverni chieftain Vercingetorix. Caesar was vastly outnumbered, pitting his 50,000 troops against anywhere from 180,000 to 330,000 Gauls. (Estimates vary widely, as they do in most accounts of ancient warfare.)

Caesar began the siege of the hill fortress in September, but before the end of that month Commius, king of the Belgic Atrebates tribe, formerly a close ally of Rome and now a key participant in the rebellion of Vercingetorix against Roman dominion in Gaul, led an attack on Caesar's position from outside the fortress while Vercingetorix himself fought from the inside. With titanic effort, the Romans managed to repulse both attacks, but on the very next day, the Gauls launched a surprise nighttime attack (battle after dark was rare in ancient warfare), stunning the Romans and pushing them back from some of their fortified lines. Thanks to Caesar's subordinates Marc Antony and Gaius Trebonius, timely Roman cavalry action prevented the breakthrough from becoming a complete and devastating rout.

Still, Caesar had suffered a setback, and by the beginning of October, the Roman besiegers were in a semi-starving condition. The Gauls, also languishing, were desperate, and on October 2, Vercingetorix's cousin Vercassivellaunus led a massive breakout assault, hurling 60,000 men against a weak point he had discovered in the Roman siege works (despite Caesar's efforts to hide it). While Vercassivellaunus pressed the assault in this sector,

Vercingetorix divided his forces and used them to attack from several directions at once.

The most Caesar believed he could hope for was to hold his siege lines until the enemy, which he knew was at least as hungry as his own army, had exhausted themselves. Caesar continually encouraged his haggard troops by riding among them in his bright scarlet cloak, long a trademark of his command.

When it seemed that his lines were about to break, Caesar rallied his men into doing precisely what he thought was impossible—mounting a counterattack. He organized thirteen cavalry cohorts—perhaps 6,000 men—to make a strike against the rear of Vercassivellaunus's 60,000. The effect of this surprise counterassault, so audacious coming from a force outnumbered ten to one, was stunning. The Gauls panicked, order instantly collapsed, and their retreat quickly became a rout. Caesar pursued as best he and his spent men could, and he did manage to exact a heavy toll on the Gauls, killing perhaps 56,000 (by some estimates 90,000), though he fell short of completely annihilating the enemy because his own troops were too depleted for sustained combat. Even so, Alesia was the last major battle of the Gallic War, and all Gaul henceforth was a province of Rome.

Invest in a scarlet cloak. Effective leadership requires a high profile. Make yourself conspicuous.

■

Lesson 90
Fight for Your Life

> "He said to his friends that he had often before struggled for
> victory, but this was the first time that he had to fight for his life."
>
> ~ Plutarch, *Life of Caesar*

Although Caesar's decisive victory at the Battle of Pharsalus in 48
BCE knocked his chief rival Pompey the Great out of the Civil War
and the victory of Caesar's forces two years later at the Battle of
Thaspsus destroyed what remained of the principal Pompeian
army, resistance to Caesar stubbornly continued in Hispania
(modern Spain and Portugal). This resistance was led by Pompey's
sons Gnaeus Pompeius and Sextus as well as General Titus
Labienus, who had been a highly trusted Caesarian general during
the Gallic War but had subsequently given his allegiance to Pompey.
During the spring of 46 BCE, the Pompeius brothers and Labienus
seized control of a large portion of Rome's Spanish colonies, forcing
Caesar to leave Rome with an expedition to reinforce the armies
loyal to him in Spain.

On March 17, 45 BCE, Caesar's forces (the Populares) met
those of Labienus and the Pompeius brothers (the Optimates) at
Munda in southern Spain. The Optimates, with six thousand
infantry and six thousand cavalry, occupied a strong position on
a hill less than a mile outside of the walls of the town of Munda
in a well-prepared defensible position. Caesar led a total of
approximately forty thousand men against about seventy thousand
Optimates. Many of the latter were highly motivated, since they had
earlier surrendered to Caesar, who pardoned them, and were well
aware that Caesar would not be so generous to them again if they
were defeated and captured.

The ensuing battle was ferocious and, for a long while,
seesawed wildly. At one point, Caesar perceived his legions faltering
and therefore dismounted his horse and waded into his forces to
rally them personally. To ensure that he would be recognized,

Caesar cast off his helmet and thus faced close combat bareheaded. He was at this point the most powerful man in the world. He had conquered Gaul, and he had defeated his rival for control of the Roman Empire. Yet now, like any common soldier, he was willing to stake his life in combat to convert defeat into victory.

His gamble succeeded. The sudden appearance of their commander was electrifying. According to eyewitnesses, not only was the incipient Roman rout stemmed, it was instantly reversed. The Tenth Legion in particular—long Caesar's special favorite—stood fast, slugged it out, and then advanced against the Optimates, who began to fall back. As Caesar's forces continued to apply pressure, the Optimate ranks panicked, discipline dissolved, and they scrambled for the rear. As often happens in battle, the collapse of the vanguard spread rearward like a contagion, and the long, hard battle ended suddenly in the general rout of the far larger enemy. By the end, the Optimates had lost a staggering thirty thousand killed, whereas Caesar's forces, having been brought to the brink of total defeat, lost perhaps a thousand.

A leader may accumulate a substantial store of motivational tools, ranging from eloquent speeches to cash bonuses, but when the stakes are at their highest, nothing is more powerful than putting your own job, cash, reputation, or future on the line. Get up from behind your desk, get out onto the shop floor, and be seen fighting for your life.

■

Lesson 91
Be Authentic

> "Thus Julius Caesar, Alexander of Macedon, and all such men and
> excellent princes always fought at the head of their own armies, always
> marched with them on foot, and always carried their own arms; if any
> of them ever lost his power, he simultaneously lost his life with it and
> died with the same *virtù* that he had displayed while he lived."
>
> ~Niccolò Machiavelli, *The Art of War*

The celebrated political philosopher of the Italian Renaissance Niccolò
Machiavelli (1469–1527) was no unabashed admirer of Julius Caesar, a
leader upon whom he blamed the destruction of the Roman Republic
to make way for the rule of hereditary emperors. Nevertheless,
Machiavelli cited Caesar, along with Alexander the Great, as one of the
rulers he called the "excellent princes" who, in everything they said and
did, revealed themselves as leaders authentic to their core.

These men possessed what Machiavelli called *virtù*, which
subsequent scholars have variously defined as courage, strength,
boldness, skill, and civic spirit, but which we may define more directly
as the very essence of leadership. For it is less important to attempt to
identify the separate ingredients of *virtù* than it is to understand that
to possess this quality requires total and complete identification of
yourself with your role as a leader. As Machiavelli explained, when
such a leader ceases to be a leader, he dies. For him, leadership and
life itself are one and the same. This is the ultimate authenticity.

"CEO" is a meaningless series of capital letters unless you
inject them with the *virtù* of your authenticity as a leader. Fight
at the head of your troops. March with them. Carry your own
arms. Make it clear to every member of your organization that
leading the enterprise is not a job you take up at nine and put
down at five, but a way of life, every hour of every day.
Authenticity does not punch a clock.

Lesson 92
Set the Bar

> "[Caesar impressed his soldiers with] his ability to endure physical
> toils that appeared to be beyond the strength of his body."
>
> ~ Plutarch, *Life of Caesar*

For Caesar, it was not enough for a commander to issue commands.
A commander had to command. He did not merely wield authority,
he *was* authority. His appearance, his actions, his very being were
living examples to his soldiers. They set the bar for the unit's
conduct, performance, and achievement.

> **Those who study and** practice leadership in a military context
> frequently speak of an officer's "command presence." Though
> commonly used, the phrase is somewhat nebulous in its
> meaning. It is best to say that it describes persuasive authority
> as a product of the persona an officer projects to his soldiers. It
> is a combination of appearance, bearing, speech, actions, and
> performance in all aspects of soldiering. In other words,
> "command presence" describes the officer as a real-time
> example of leadership. Caesar clearly mastered the art of
> command presence. In everything he did and said, he set the
> bar of performance for his enterprise. Leadership is not just a
> fulltime job. It is a way of being in the world.

■

A Caesarian Timeline

All dates are BCE.

100

Gaius Julius Caesar is born in the shabby Subura neighborhood of
Rome, the son of Aurelia Cotta and Gaius Julius Caesar, a praetor.
Although the family is patrician, it is no longer wealthy, and it is
also politically identified with the populist Populares political
faction rather than with the noble Optimates.

85

Gaius Julius Caesar, Caesar's father, dies. Shortly after this, Caesar
is betrothed to (and may even have married) a wealthy young
woman named Cossutia.

84

After the betrothal (or marriage) to Cossutia is broken off, Caesar
marries Cornelia, daughter of Lucius Cornelius Cinna, a leader of
the Populares.

ca. 80

The Optimate dictator Lucius Cornelius Sulla spares Caesar from
his bloody political purges, but strips him of his inheritance, dowry,
and a minor priesthood. When he orders him to divorce Cornelia,
Caesar instead defiantly joins the staff of Marcus Thermus, a
military legate (general), and serves in Roman Asia.

80–79

For distinguishing himself at the siege and Battle of Mytilene, Caesar is awarded the Civic Crown; however, he also becomes the subject of a rumor that he had a sexual liaison with King Nicomedes of Bithniya. The rumor would dog him all his life.

78

With Sulla's death this year, Caesar returns to Rome and commences a career as an advocate (lawyer).

75

Seeking advanced study in rhetoric and oratory, Caesar takes ship for Rhodes to study with Apollonius Molon, a renowned rhetorician. Kidnapped en route by Cilician pirates, he is held for ransom. Caesar boldly takes control of the situation, raises the ransom, obtains his release, recruits and commands a naval flotilla, locates and captures the pirates, and arranges for their crucifixion.

72

Back in Rome, Caesar is elected military tribune.

69

Both his much-loved aunt, Julia, and his wife, Cornelia, die this year, occasioning from Caesar two notable public funeral orations, which win him public sympathy, admiration, and support.

68–67

Caesar is elected quaestor (mainly a supervisor of financial affairs), obtains a Senate seat, and marries Pompeia, granddaughter of Sulla.

65

Elected curule aedile, Caesar is (among other things) responsible for organizing and managing public games and festivals, on which he spends staggering amounts of borrowed money in order to curry favor with the people.

63

Using bribery and other methods (thereby multiplying his already staggering debt), Caesar is elected pontifex maximus (head priest of the College of Pontiffs).

62

Caesar is elected praetor (urban magistrate). After Pompeia is implicated in an affair with another man (who is also guilty of having crashed a sacred all-female Bona Dea ceremony), Caesar divorces her, reportedly remarking, "the wife of Caesar must be above suspicion."

61

Caesar serves as propraetor (military commander and magistrate) in Hispania Ulterior (Farther Spain).

60

On his return from Spain, Caesar joins forces with Pompey (Gnaeus Pompeius) and Marcus Licinius Crassus in what modern historians call the First Triumvirate.

59

Thanks in large measure to the triumvirate alliance, Caesar is elected consul. He marries off his only daughter, Julia, to Pompey to ratify and reinforce their alliance, and he himself marries Calpurnia Pisonis, daughter of a popularist leader. As consul, Caesar promotes his agenda as well as those of both Pompey and

Crassus. His own most important legislation is a radical land reform law that allots public Roman lands throughout Italy to dispossessed farmers and discharged legion veterans. The law changes the social structure of Rome.

58

Appointed governor of Cisalpine and Transalpine Gaul, Caesar devotes the next nine years to pacifying, consolidating, and greatly expanding this portion of the Roman Republic's empire. A masterpiece of military strategy and tactics as well as civil governance, the conquest of Gaul not only brings Rome great wealth and changes the course of Greco-Roman and Western history, it positions Caesar for ultimate power in Rome.

54

Caesar leads his first expedition/raid into Britain. Crassus is killed in battle with the Parthians, and Julia (Caesar's daughter and Pompey's wife) dies in childbirth; these events accelerate the dissolution of the faltering alliance between Caesar and Pompey, who has increasingly connected himself with the Optimates and the Senate against Caesar.

52

Amid rioting in Rome, Pompey is elected sole consul. From this position of absolute power, he aligns himself forthrightly with the Optimates and against Caesar.

51

Caesar publishes *The Gallic War*, which chronicles his conquests; the Optimates, however, move to cut short his governorship of Gaul.

50

The Senate orders Caesar to lay down his command, but permits Pompey to retain his army. Caesar responds to the Senate with a proposal that he and Pompey be required to lay down their commands simultaneously. Professing offense at the insolent tone of Caesar's message, the Senate declares that Caesar will be branded as a public enemy if he fails to lay down his command as ordered.

49

Caesar leads the vanguard of his army into northern Italy and crosses the Rubicon River into Roman Italy, thereby violating Roman law and initiating civil war.

48

Pompey builds up his forces in Greece, and an outnumbered Caesar battles him there in a war that culminates at Pharsalus on August 9. Although he is outnumbered more than two to one, Caesar defeats Pompey, who abandons his army and flees to Egypt, where Ptolemy XIII rules jointly with his sister/wife Cleopatra. When Caesar, in pursuit of Pompey, lands at Alexandria, he is presented with Pompey's severed head—Ptolemy having ordered his assassination in a vain attempt to curry favor with Caesar.

48-47

Caesar unites with Cleopatra both politically and sexually (if not quite romantically) to defeat Ptolemy XIII in battle on March 26. Caesar departs Egypt June 23, having established Cleopatra as Egypt's ruler, subject to Rome. A son is born to Cleopatra shortly after he leaves. Naming him Caesarion, she claims that Caesar is his father.

47–46

From Egypt, Caesar travels to Asia Minor, where he conducts a lightning campaign against a rebellious King Pharnaces of Pontus (on the southern coast of the Black Sea, today in Turkey). Caesar sums up his victory in one of the most brilliantly succinct sentences ever penned in any language: "*Veni, vidi, vici*" ("I came, I saw, I conquered"). Arriving in Rome in October, he makes short work of a mutiny among his legions, and then sails with them to Africa to defeat Pompeian/Optimate diehards at the Battle of Thapsus on April 6, 46.

46

Caesar again returns to Rome, where he marches in an unprecedented series of four triumphs, commemorating his victories in Gaul, Egypt, Asia Minor, and Africa. Establishing Cleopatra and Caesarion in his villa outside of the city of Rome, he sets about instituting a program of sweeping reforms that included (among other things) resolving the Roman debt crisis, resettling masses of veterans without displacing others, introducing the Julian calendar, regulating the distribution of grain, nurturing a Roman middle class, and expanding the Senate. Predictably, the populist direction of these reforms outrages and alienates the nobles, including the many Optimates who have long opposed and fought him but to whom Caesar grants a blanket amnesty.

45

Pompey's sons Gnaeus and Sextus lead a revolt in Spain, which Caesar puts down with his victory at the Battle of Munda on March 17 (Gnaeus Pompey is killed, but Sextus escapes and becomes a pirate leader). Returned to Rome in October, Caesar upsets many by celebrating his victory over Gnaeus Pompey with a triumph. Roman custom reserves triumphs for victories against foreigners, not fellow Romans. Also, despite enacting so many

enlightened reforms, Caesar assumes more and more absolute
powers and begins to encourage a quasi-religious personality cult
to develop around him.

44

After being named *dictator perpetuus* ("dictator in perpetuity"),
Caesar wears purple—emblem of royalty—on February 15, at the
feast of Lupercalia; however, when his friend and ally Marc Antony
offers him a diadem, Caesar throws it into the crowd, proclaiming
that Jupiter is the only king of the Romans. A month later, on
March 15 (the Ides of March), some sixty assassins, foremost
among whom are Marcus Junius Brutus, Gaius Cassius Longinus,
Decimus Brutus Albinus, and Gaius Trebonius, stab Caesar
twenty-three times.

Further Reading

Batstone, William, and Cynthia Damon. *Caesar's Civil War*. New York: Oxford University Press, 2006.

Burns, Thomas S. *Rome and the Barbarians, 100 B.C.–A.D. 400*. Baltimore: Johns Hopkins University Press, 2003.

Caesar, Gaius Julius. *Civil Wars*, translated by A. G. Peskett. Cambridge, MA: Harvard University Press, 1914.

——. *The Gallic War*, translated by H. J. Edwards. Cambridge, MA: Harvard University Press, 1917.

Cunliffe, Barry. *The Ancient Celts*. Oxford, UK: Oxford University Press, 1997.

Dando-Collins, Stephen. *Caesar's Legion*. Hoboken, NJ: John Wiley & Sons, 2002.

Dodge, Theodore Ayrault. *Caesar: A History of the Art of War among the Romans Down to the End of the Roman Empire, with a Detailed Account of the Campaigns of Caius Julius Caesar*. 1892, reprint ed. London: Greenhill Books, 1995.

Everitt, Anthony. *Cicero: The Life and Times of Rome's Greatest Politician*. New York: Random House, 2001.

Fields, Nic. *Julius Caesar: Leadership, Strategy, Conflict*. Oxford, UK: Osprey, 2010.

Freeman, Philip. *Julius Caesar*. New York: Simon and Schuster, 2008.

Fuller, J. F. C. *Julius Caesar: Man, Soldier, and Tyrant.* New Brunswick, NJ: De Capo Press, 1965.

Gelzer, Matthias. *Caesar: Politician and Statesman.* Cambridge, MA: Harvard University Press, 1968.

Goldsworthy, Adrian. *Caesar: Life of a Colossus.* New Haven, CT: Yale University Press, 2006.

———. *Caesar's Civil War.* Oxford, UK: Osprey Publishing, 2002.

———. *The Complete Roman Army.* London: Thames and Hudson, 2003.

Grant, Michael. *Julius Caesar.* London: Chancellor Press, 1969.

Gulliver, Kate. *Caesar's Gallic Wars.* Oxford, UK: Osprey Publishing, 2002.

Holland, Tom. *Rubicon: The Last Years of the Roman Republic.* New York: Doubleday, 2003.

Kamm, Anthony. *Julius Caesar: A Life.* London: Routledge, 2006.

Kruta, Venceslas, ed. *The Celts.* London: Hachette Illustrated, 2004.

Le Glay, Marcel, Jean-Louis Voisin, and Yann Le Bohec. *A History of Rome.* Oxford, UK: Blackwell, 1996.

Lendon, J. E. *Soldiers and Ghosts: A History of Battle in Classical Antiquity.* New Haven, CT: Yale University Press, 2005.

Matyszak, Philip. *Chronicle of the Roman Republic.* London: Thames & Hudson, 2003.

Meier, Christian. *Caesar: A Biography.* New York: Basic Books, 1982.

Osgood, Josiah. *Caesar's Legacy: Civil War and the Emergence of the Roman Empire.* Cambridge, MA: Cambridge University Press, 2006.

Parenti, Michael. *The Assassination of Julius Caesar: A People's History of Ancient Rome.* New York: The New Press, 2003.

Powell, Anton, and Kathryn Welch, eds. *Julius Caesar as Artful Reporter: The War Commentaries as Political Instruments.* London: Duckworth, 1998.

Riggsby, Andrew M. *Caesar in Gaul and Rome: War in Words.* Austin: University of Texas Press, 2006.

Lesson Index

the fortification which he had made, and himself hurried by forced marches into Italy. There he enrolled two legions.

troops unarmed and unprepared, he placed all the timber felled on the side towards
the enemy, and also piled it as a rampart on both flanks. With incredible rapidity,
a great space was cleared in a few days, until the enemy's cattle and the rearward
of their baggage were in our keeping, while [the enemy] themselves sought the
denser forests.

3 NEGOTIATION AND PERSUASION

4 TACTICS AND TECHNIQUES

Lesson 49

Choose Your Battlefield 124

He chose a ground . . . naturally suitable and appropriate . . .

Lesson 50

Rally Your Centurions 126

He went forward into the first line, and, calling on the centurions by name, and cheering on the rank and file, he bade them advance.

Lesson 51

Pitch In 127

His coming brought hope to the troops and renewed their spirit; each man of his own accord, in sight of the commander-in-chief, desperate as his own case might be, was fain to do his utmost. So the onslaught of the enemy was checked a little.

Lesson 52

Confess Weakness and Learn to Be Strong 129

When our own fleet encountered these ships [of the Gauls and Celts] it proved its superiority only in speed and oarsmanship; in all other respects, having regard to the locality and force of the tempests, the others were more suitable and adaptable.

Lesson 53

Attack for Effect 131

And as all the hope of the Gallic ships lay in their sails and tackle, when these were torn away all chance of using their ships was taken away also.

Lesson 54

Always Play to Your Advantage 133

The rest of the conflict was a question of courage, in which our own troops easily had the advantage.

Lesson 55

Build Better Ships 134

He set forth the plan and pattern of the new ships.

Lesson 67

Refuse Victimhood 158

[Caesar] held them [his pirate captors] in such disdain that whenever he lay down to sleep he would send and order them to stop talking. For thirty-eight days, as if the men were not his watchers, but his royal bodyguard, he shared in their sports and exercises with great unconcern.

Lesson 68

Take Every Opportunity to Broadcast Your Brand 161

By . . . constant renewal of the good report of brave men, the celebrity of those who performed noble deeds is rendered immortal, while at the same time the fame of those who did good service to their country becomes known to the people and a heritage for future generations.

Lesson 69

Remove Failure as an Option 162

Caesar first had his own horse and then those of all others sent out of sight, thus to equalize the danger of all and to take away the hope of flight.

Lesson 70

Use Competitive Motivation 164

Even if no one else follows, I shall march with the Tenth Legion alone; I have no doubt of its allegiance.

Lesson 71

Be There: Everywhere 165

Caesar gave the necessary commands, and then ran down in a chance direction to harangue the troops . . . . He started off at once in the other direction to give a like harangue. . . . The time was so short, the temper of the enemy so ready for conflict.

Lesson 72

Send a Strong Message 168

He decided that their punishment must be the more severe in order that the privilege of deputies might be more carefully preserved by natives for the future. He therefore put the whole of their senate to the sword, and sold the rest of the men as slaves.

Lesson 73
To Be Proactive Be Predictive 169

Although Caesar had not yet learnt their designs, yet the misfortune of his ships and the fact that the chiefs had broken off the surrender of hostages led him to suspect that events would turn out as they did; and therefore he prepared means to meet any emergency.

Lesson 74
Go Back to Italy 171

. . . to go to Italy, as it was his practice every year to do . . .

Lesson 75
Avoid Relying on the Moment 172

[Titurius] ran hither and thither posting cohorts, yet even this he did in timid fashion and with all judgment evidently gone, as generally happens when men are forced to decide in the moment of action.

Lesson 76
Don't Be Damned by a Damn Good Defense 173

It diminished the hope of our own troops and made the enemy keener for the fight, since the movement could not but betray the greatest apprehension and despair.

Lesson 77
Replace Blame with Praise 176

The next day he [Caesar] held a parade [military review] and set forth all that had occurred, cheering and encouraging the troops, and admonishing them to bear with the greater equanimity the loss incurred [earlier] through the fault and foolhardiness of a general [Lucius Aurunculeius Cotta and/or Quintus Titurius Sabinus], inasmuch as by the goodness of the immortal gods and by their own valour the misfortune had been made good, leaving to the enemy no lasting joy, to themselves no long-enduring grief.

6 THE VALOR PROPOSITION

Index

Sterling Books by Alan Axelrod